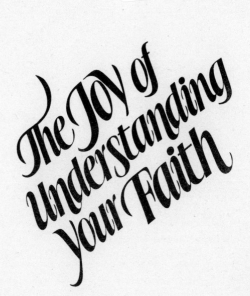

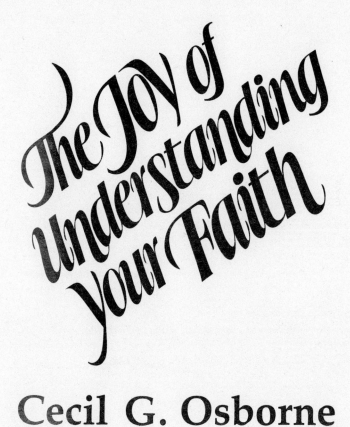

The Joy of Understanding Your Faith

Cecil G. Osborne

Abingdon Press
Nashville

THE JOY OF UNDERSTANDING YOUR FAITH

Copyright © 1983 by Abingdon Press

Library of Congress Cataloging in Publication Data

OSBORNE, CECIL G.
 The joy of understanding your faith.
 1. Apologetics—20th century. I. Title.
 BT1102.O8   1983   230   83-3808

ISBN 0-687-20594-8 (pbk.)

Unless otherwise noted, all Scripture quotations are from the Revised
Standard Version of the Bible, copyrighted 1946, 1952, © 1971, 1973 by the
Division of Christian Education of the National Council of Churches of
Christ in the U.S.A., and used by permission. Quotations noted TLB are
from *The Living Bible*, copyright © 1971 Tyndale House Publishers,
Wheaton, Illinois. Used by permission. Those noted NEB are from The
New English Bible. © the Delegates of the Oxford University Press and the
Syndics of the Cambridge University Press 1961, 1970. Reprinted by
permission.

See also page 191 for continuation of credits.

MANUFACTURED BY THE PARTHENON PRESS AT
NASHVILLE, TENNESSEE, UNITED STATES OF AMERICA

To Isobel,
my wife for fifty-seven happy years,
who now inhabits the other dimension of time and
space we call heaven, and manifests there her endless
love and patience. She now knows with
deep certainty what we perceive here imperfectly;
and to my Yokefellows who struggle to reach the goal
of unconditional love.

Dr. Cecil G. Osborne may be contacted at the following address:

Yokefellows, Inc.
Burlingame Counseling Center
19 Park Road
Burlingame, CA 94010

Contents

Introduction

This book was written in response to hundreds of letters from perplexed, frustrated Christians who have read some of my previous books. Here are a few excerpts from some typical letters:

"My wife and I both love the Lord a great deal, and are committed to serving him the rest of our lives. We are active in a 'Spirit-filled' church, where we are engaged in a specialized ministry.

"From all outward appearances we have the world by the tail, but, Dr. Osborne, I am tormented daily by fear, frustration, and a nagging lump in my throat when I try to talk to people. I have read a lot of how-to books, and they leave me frustrated."

He wonders, of course, why his physical and emotional symptoms persist, despite earnest prayer.

A young woman writes: "How do I really get to know God? How can I get to the place where I love him? I have been taught that I need him, but it hasn't had any effect on my life. One reason I have difficulty in being a dedicated Christian is because they tell me I must put away all of my own desires; but I do want to know and love him."

Many of the people who write me say that they have

been told that they lack faith; that they must pray harder, or confess their sins more earnestly. This, of course, simply compounds their feelings of guilt and unworthiness.

A woman suffering from cancer said that she was visited daily by earnest, devout Christian friends who prayed with her and assured her that if she had enough faith she could be healed. As a result of this she went into a deep depression lasting several years. Her friends succeeded in convincing her that the fault was her lack of faith. She felt a total failure as a Christian.

A missionary writes: "I have suffered most of my life from excessive fear and anxiety, as well as from a number of phobias. I feel that these symptoms are a negation of my faith and a hindrance in my work. Why do I suffer from these symptoms?"

Some of the letters run to five, ten, twelve, or more pages. One young woman wrote: "I was raised in a Christian home by two stable and loving parents. My father was a perfectionist, my mother stern and demanding. She was whining and critical most of the time. I accepted the Lord and it made a difference, but my feelings of anxiety, fear, and guilt are still with me. I feel rejected and hopeless." She wonders why her faith is not relieving her terrible sense of desolation.

A man writes at considerable length: "My life was a complete shambles. I was an alcoholic, but for nine years I have been free of alcoholism. I *know*, intellectually, that God loves me, but I have a hard time *believing* it at a feeling level. I have a poor self-image. I study the Bible, and need the peace I read about. How do I get it? How soon can I be accepted for Primal Integration therapy at your Center?"

Another writes: "I'm a born-again Christian, but

have only fleeting moments of the abundant life the Bible speaks about. There seems to be a great wall between God and me."

Some write of marital difficulties, fears and phobias, a desolating sense of loneliness, a feeling that there must be something wrong with them if they cannot find the "peace that passes understanding."

One earnest Christian woman writes: "My emotional problems are too deeply rooted to simply pray them away. My husband and I want to serve Jesus more than anything else in the world, but how can we give him something we don't have? We will sacrifice anything to have you work with us. We have no money, but will sell all we have in order to receive the kind of therapy you provide at your Center . . . as far back as I can remember I have hated myself. Can you help me?"

And on and on and on. They are asking, "What's wrong with me that I don't have more faith? Are the Bible's promises true? Why do decent, earnest Christians suffer, while many non-Christians seem to be trouble free?" Some say that they have tried to read the Bible but it makes no sense to them, yet they want to believe.

They ask, in one form or another, such questions as these:

Why do the righteous suffer?
How can I find the will of God for my life?
Why are my prayers unanswered?
Is the Bible really the inspired word of God?
How can Jesus atone for my sins today when he
     lived two thousand years ago?

Why can't the church meet more of my personal
   needs?
Are heaven and hell realities?
Since I believe all the fundamentals of the faith and
   try to live a good Christian life, why do I have to
   endure so much sorrow and disappointment?

I don't profess to have all the answers. Some may
find my explanations unacceptable, but if this book
stimulates your thinking and helps you formulate a
deeper faith in Christ, I shall be rewarded.

1

Creation

Education is the process of moving from cocksure ignorance to thoughtful uncertainty.
— *T. H. Bell, U. S. Commissioner of Education*

An Incredibly Vast Universe

In our particular corner of the universe there are at least one thousand million (1,000,000,000), or one billion, galaxies with a general structure similar to our own.

One eminent astronomer estimates that in the observable universe there must be a trillion stars with planets conducive to life of some sort. The creator of this incredibly vast universe is certainly not an eight-foot God somewhere out in space. "You can't shake hands with the One who created *that*," one astronomer said, gazing through his telescope.

The most recently discovered quasar—the name stands for quasi-stellar radio source—is about eight billion light years away, which means that any light from the object, traveling at the speed of 186,000 miles per second, takes eight billion years to reach us. This implies an incomprehensibly vast universe; yet, for all we know, that distant source of radio waves may be fairly close compared to others still beyond the reach of our most powerful telescopes.

How much is a billion? A man gave his wife one million dollars. He told her to go out and spend a thousand dollars a day. She did, and three years later she returned to tell him that the money was all gone. She wanted more. He then gave her one billion dollars and told her to go out and spend a thousand dollars a day. She didn't come back for three thousand years.

It is too easy to limit one's concept of God. A man in clerical garb took his seat on a plane and turned to greet the man seated next to him. That rather serious-looking gentleman said, "My friend, I see that you are a clergyman, and I would like to make it clear that I do not wish to discuss theology, or any topic related to religion. I am an astronomer, and my religious faith is summed up in the command, 'Do to others what you would have them do to you' " (Matt. 7:12 NIV).

The clergyman replied gently, "I am glad that you've found a satisfying religious concept. I happen to have found a very simple but meaningful concept of astronomy. It is summed up in the phrase, 'Twinkle, twinkle, little star.' "

The sum total of God's truth cannot be expressed in a single phrase any more than the vastness of his universe can be contained in a child's wonderment over a twinkling star.

One school of astronomers postulates the idea that the universe is infinite—that there are conceivably as many stars as there are grains of sand on all the shores of all the oceans of the earth, multiplied by millions. Some believe that the universe is expanding, and that it will go on expanding forever. Others tend to think that in several billion years it will cease to expand and gradually contract to become, ultimately, a single gigantic mass, then explode in another "big bang," such as the one which presumably began what we think of as creation.

In our galaxy alone there are something like eight hundred thousand million—eight hundred billion—(800,000,000,000) stars in what we call the Milky Way. Astronomers theorize that there may be one billion planets in the Milky Way capable of supporting some kind of long-term evolution.

While the futile quarrel between evolutionists and creationists has largely subsided, a few contenders here and there still try to keep the argument going. Without fully understanding the basic contention of Charles Darwin, some people think of him as an atheist who taught that we descended from monkeys. He was not an atheist, nor did he contend that humans descended from apes. In fact, Darwin wrote in his *Origin of Species* (6th ed.): "There is grandeur in this view of life, with its several powers, having been originally breathed by the Creator into a few forms, or into one; that whilst this planet has gone circling on according to the fixed law of gravity, from a simple beginning endless forms most beautiful and won-derful have been, and are being, evolved."

The evolutionary hypothesis is still only a theory. If some people find more comfort in the idea that God created the earth, man, and hundreds of thousands of other species, in six twenty-four-hour days, there is no particular reason to abandon that view. Our relationship with God is not affected either way. Most theologians, however, accept the evolutionary hypothesis as being the most probable means of creation employed by God.

Religion for the Perplexed

"Christians must realize that the scriptures do not require us to believe in six twenty-four-hour days of creation," writes Dr. Davis A. Young, an eminent evangelical Christian scientist in *Christianity and the Age of the Earth* (Zondervan, 1982). He continues:

There is legitimate internal biblical evidence to indicate that the days of creation may have been indefinite periods of time. . . . Why . . . are some Christians so rigidly dogmatic about matters on which the Bible itself is not dogmatic? . . . Christians should not paint themselves into a corner by being more rigid than the Bible. . . . A Christian should not be bothered by the idea that the Earth is extremely old. He should not feel that Christianity is threatened, or that the veracity of the Bible is undermined because the evidence of nature suggests the antiquity of our planet.

On the other hand,

Chandra Wickramasinghe, a distinguished astrophysicist from University College, Cardiff, Wales, . . . and his older, more eminent collaborator, British astronomer, Sir Fred Hoyle, both former disbelievers in a life-creating God, are now persuaded that such a God exists. Not only that, they believe that the existence of a creator can be established by mathematics, with a probability greater than $10^{40,000}$ (1 followed by 40,000 zeros) to 1. . . . Natural laws cannot account for life's origins and that Darwinian natural selection cannot explain its development.

The last big leap, from beast to human is so enormous that Hoyle cannot conceive of it as being the result of

DNA replication errors. He says there is no way a Darwinian struggle for survival can explain "the emergence of a Mozart, a Shakespeare, or a Karl Frederick Gauss" (*Discover*, March 1982).

Let's take a look at one of the most remarkable aspects of creation—the process by which a single fertilized ovum becomes, in the course of nine months, a human child. Almost as soon as it is formed, the cell begins to divide, first in two, then each succeeding cell in two again, and so on. At the outset the cells in the cluster are—or seem to be—all alike, but slowly differentiation begins to appear and primitive structures are created from which other organs will form. It is a process of the most amazing coordination, in which cells go to their appointed places at the right time and develop the right properties for carrying out the function of that part of the structure. All the billions of cells have come from one single progenitor, yet in the end

some will have changed their stuff and become rigid bone, or harder still, the enamel of a tooth; some become fluid as water, so as to flow along tubes too fine for the eye to see. Some are clear as glass, some black. Some become factories of a furious chemistry, some become inert as death. Some become engines of mechanical pull, some scaffoldings of static support, some a system transmitting electrical signs. (Sir Charles Sherrington, Gifford Lectures, 1937-38)

How does heredity work? By what divine mechanism does a child inherit characteristics of its parents? What is the blueprint or master plan for creating a new human being? A person is a complicated creation, and tens of thousands of instructions are required to build one. How can all those instructions be packed into a tiny egg a few thousandths of an inch in size?

In his review of the book *The Eighth Day of Creation*, by Horace Freeland Judson, Robert Jastrow writes:

Biologists know exactly where in the little egg the instructions are stored. They reside in a molecule called DNA, which sits at the center of every living cell. . . . A DNA molecule in a human cell contains about a million "words." Each molecule is one volume in the genetic library.

Every living organism—a tree, a mouse, a human being—has a library of instructions for making copies of itself printed on the steps of those spiral staircases. (*Psychology Today*, September 1979)

The infinitely small DNA molecule, the library of codes, determines the physical characteristics, the color, shape, and texture of a million or more different physical, mental, and emotional traits. It is the ultimate in miniaturization. The DNA molecule in a human being is composed of roughly five billion nucleotides. Since there are four different kinds of nucleotides, that means that each molecule contains *twenty billion* bits of information.

A human being is a pretty complex organism. For instance, one square inch of human skin contains the following:

78 nerves
650 sweat glands
19 to 20 blood vessels
78 sensory apparatuses
1,300 nerve endings to record pain
19,000 sensory cells at the end of nerve fibers

160 to 165 pressure apparatuses for the sense of touch
95 to 100 sebaceous glands
65 hairs and muscles
19,500,000,000 cells

Was Creation a Fortuitous Accident?

Very few atheists are around these days, so what follows is not an effort to convert any actual or potential atheists, or to beat a dead lion. Rather, it is a means of reminding ourselves of the grandeur of God's creative plan.

There is an old theory that if an infinite number of monkeys pounded on an infinite number of type-writers, they would eventually, inadvertently, crank out a great work of literature, such as *Hamlet*. However, a recent computer analysis of this proposition by Dr. William R. Bennett, Jr., a professor of physics at Yale, indicates that it would still take a trillion times longer than the universe has been in existence before the monkeys would get even the single line, "To be or not to be, that is the question."

For me to believe that this universe, with its staggering complexity, could have evolved by accident would require vastly more faith than it does to believe in a creator. It is axiomatic that a design requires a designer, a building implies a builder, a creation demands a creator.

Dr. Wernher von Braun, pioneer NASA scientist, once said, "Anything as well ordered and perfectly created as is our earth and universe must have a Maker, a Master Designer. Anything so orderly, so perfect, so precisely balanced, so majestic as this creation, can only be the product of a Divine idea. . . . There must be a Maker; there can be no other way."

What are the probabilities that this universe, and man, are the result of blind chance? A mathematician has pointed out that if you take ten pennies, numbering them from one to ten, and put them in your pocket, the chances of drawing them out in sequence are one in 3,638,800. In that little experiment we are dealing with only ten factors. When we consider the fact that our universe is billions of times more complex, the chance that even a human cell could evolve by accident is roughly equivalent to the probability that an explosion in a printing plant would result in a printed copy of an encyclopedia.

Approximately one hundred and fifty thousand red blood cells are born each second, and an equal number die. If the number of new cells being born were one hundredth of 1 percent less, death would result. Who engineered this incredible process?

This vast universe consists of billions of different objects, in various shapes and forms; yet, incredibly enough, they are all made from ninety simple but unseen elements in nature. These elements consist of atoms, which are made up of electrical charges. All matter, then, is simply an arrangement of positive and negative charges of electricity. Matter is energy falling ceaselessly into form, at the command of the One who said, "Let there be light; and there was light" (Gen. 1:3).

If it is true that what we call matter is simply energy falling into form, then we can begin to understand a little more clearly the statement in Hebrews, "By faith we understand that the world was created by the word of God, so that what is seen was *made out of things which do not appear*"—those things that are invisible (Heb. 11:3, italics added).

The first law of thermodynamics states in essence that energy can be transformed in various ways, but cannot be created or destroyed. Energy, power, is transformed into matter according to divine purpose. Thus we can say, with reverence and awe, "God, All Mighty." The kingdom, and the power, and the glory are all his. They are manifestations of his nature.

God has turned this little planet over to us. "Take it," he said to Adam (humankind). "Have dominion over it. Run it, rule, it, see what you can do with it." And we have done some wonderful and some frightening things to God's world.

The pollution of oceans and lakes and the atmosphere, the devastation of our natural resources, the thousand and one wars, and the Holocaust are man-made horrors.

It is simple to find the guilty party. We can blame someone or something else without the slightest difficulty. It is not the establishment, or rebellious youth, or the church, or parents, or the Pentagon. It is the fault of man, the human race. These things have taken place because of our sin and guilt. There is no one to blame. We are all involved in it. If you dislike the term "original sin," call it corporate guilt, or the ongoing willfulness of humans who refuse to get into harmony with the universal, cosmic laws and who violate them to their own destruction. Pogo, in one of the comic strips, says, "We have met the enemy and he is *us*."

In 1843 it took at least three months to travel from Chicago to San Francisco. In 1943 it took about three days and nights by train. Now it takes a little over three hours. Yet we humans are no different fundamentally—physically, mentally, morally—than

Abraham, when he came out of his ancient Sumerian civilization at the command of God, to seek a new home. It is fascinating to speculate as to how, living in a pagan society, Abraham made the transcendent discovery of the one true, living God and learned to walk with him in intimate fellowship.

Proving the Existence of God

A college student once asked me if I could prove that there is a God. I told him that I knew of no way to prove the existence of God. "However," I said, "I can tell you how you can find out for yourself, but I doubt if you will attempt it." He insisted that he was determined to know if there is a God and would do anything I suggested if it would result in his knowing for certain that God existed. I knew the kind of life he was leading, and had reason to doubt his sincerity, but I said, "This will sound so simple that you may reject it, but I promise you that if you will follow a simple formula for thirty days you will have your answer."

"I will do anything to find out. I must know!" he said.

"All right," I told him, "then say slowly and thoughtfully, five times a day for thirty days: 'O God, if there is a God, reveal yourself to me.' "

He looked disappointed, because he had expected some complex, logical, or philosophical formula, but he agreed to try it. A day or two later when I met him, he started to pass me without speaking. I touched his arm and asked, "How is your experiment going?" He was hostile. "I won't do it! It's ridiculous to go around saying anything like that. I won't do it!" He walked away looking grim.

The reason for his refusal was quite clearly pointed up by Aldous Huxley in *Ends and Means* (Harper & Brothers, 1937):

I had motives for not wanting the world to have meaning; consequently I assumed that it had none, and was able . . . to find satisfying reasons for this assumption.

For myself, as no doubt for most of my contemporaries, the philosophy of meaninglessness was essentially an instrument of liberation from . . . a certain system of morality. We objected to morality because it interfered with our sexual freedom. . . .

Similar tactics had been adopted during the eighteenth century and for the same reasons. . . . The chief reason for being "philosophical" was that one might be free from prejudices—above all, prejudices of a *sexual* nature.

The college student didn't want to admit the possibility that there could be a God, because it would mean two things for him which he could not accept: he would have to admit that there is Someone to whom he would have to bow, and that there is a moral law in the universe. Because of the kind of life he insisted on living, and his own egocentricity, this was unthinkable.

Robinson Crusoe, alone—as he thought—on his tiny island, saw a footprint in the sand one day, and was startled by the sudden knowledge that someone else was on the island. He was not alone! He had not yet seen another person and had no way of knowing what he or she was like, but that human footprint in the sand was irrefutable evidence. Someone was with him on his island.

We are not alone on our island planet. There is a Presence, invisible, but manifested in a thousand wondrous ways, supremely in Jesus, who said, "He who has seen me has seen the Father" (John 14:9*b*).

2

Sin, Suffering, and Sorrow

Man is the only animal that laughs and weeps, for he is the only animal that is struck by the difference between what things are, and what they ought to be.
—*William Hazlitt*

I doubt if anyone these days, after two world wars, and the constant revelation of new atrocities, is inclined to dispute the statement that "all have sinned and fall short of the glory of God" (Rom. 3:23). At the same time, after more than forty years of counseling, and thousands of hours of listening to people reliving in Primal Integration* sessions the traumas of childhood, I am firmly convinced that most of us are more sinned against than we are sinners. But let's look first at the reality and all pervasiveness of sin.

Would you think that an enormously successful executive, earning three hundred thousand dollars a year, would steal? The ex-president of Columbia Pictures, David Begelman, was credited with saving

---

*Primal Integration is a new and remarkably effective process whereby the repressed emotional hurts of childhood are relived, and thus discharging the encapsulated fear, anxiety, depression, and anger that are the root cause of neurosis in the adult.

Columbia Pictures from bankruptcy. He was the most powerful man in the motion picture industry. Yet he stole large amounts of money from his company. "There were no personal financial pressures," he said. After being fired from his position, and fined five thousand dollars by the court, he said, "Clearly, there were forces at work within me that I was not consciously aware of. The problems that were seething within me were coming to a point. I was enjoying my greatest professional success. This success, from my rather neurotic viewpoint, required me to start punishing myself for (what I felt was) my undeserved success" (*San Francisco Chronicle*, November 11, 1979). He learned something of his unconscious motivation as the result of twenty-one months of psychotherapy.

His problem is called psychic masochism, the unconscious will to be punished. Since he felt unworthy of the success he had attained, he sought some way to defeat or punish himself.

Obviously this explanation does not justify his dishonesty; yet, considering the fact that masochism is one of the most difficult neuroses to eradicate, it has a bearing on his conduct.

Although David Begelman stole partially out of greed and out of a masochistic need to be punished, millions of employees steal simply because they have a large streak of dishonesty in them.

It is reported that employees in American businesses steal between nine and ten billion dollars annually. Half of this total is theft in cash and merchandise from retail establishments. The remainder is lost through kickbacks, bribery, theft of time, and loss of corporate secrets. Thefts of merchandise

[25]

alone amount to 5 percent of the yearly sales of American retail establishments. The stores' own employees steal three times as much as do shoplifters.

This type of dishonesty is the result, in most cases, of a deliberate attempt to get something for nothing, to rip off the firm. The rationalization is often that "it's a big firm; they'll never miss it." Actually they don't. The loss is passed on to the consumer, who pays a higher price for the merchandise. It's another indication of the truth that "all have sinned."

Conflict of Ideals and Performance

Often there is little connection between doctrine and performance, either in religion or politics. For instance, Richard Nixon, accepting the Republican presidential nomination in 1968, said, "Let us begin by committing ourselves to the truth and to live the truth."

I am convinced that Richard Nixon meant every word he said at the time. I do not presume to judge the day-by-day steps that led to his downfall. And when I contemplate that lonely man, whose culpability is revealed for all the world and future generations to see, the only emotion I can feel is one of compassion. He blew it. But then, so have I, in one way or another.

Can you say that you have always been true to your highest ideals? That you have in every instance acted with integrity? That you have without exception told the truth? If you can answer yes to those questions, you are either a very confused person, or else you deserve to have a place in the stained-glass windows of our greatest cathedral, perhaps a bit higher than the figures of the saints, who, without exception, admittedly failed at some point.

The Apollo 8 moon rocket had 5.5 million parts. Even if all of them functioned with a 99.9 percent reliability, there would have been 5,600 defective parts and enough malfunctions to cancel the flight. We expect, and are able to produce, perfection in our machines; but as yet we humans cannot attain perfection.

I made that statement during an address at a seminar once. The host pastor interrupted with considerable agitation. He said, "No, that isn't right! I belong to a denomination that believes we can attain such perfection." I said, "When you do achieve perfection, you will be the first since Jesus. I want to know about it when it happens." No, we humans cannot expect it of ourselves. Working toward wholeness is commendable, expecting to achieve the ideal is unrealistic.

One reason, I believe, that God can accept and forgive us is that *he accepts responsibility for our being born into a world* where we are contaminated by a faulty society from the moment of birth. He understands all the forces that mold us and loves us because we are a part of him.

Plato in the dialogue *Phaedrus* likens the human soul to a chariot drawn by two horses—one black and one white—pulling in different directions and weakly controlled by the charioteer.

Something of this nature must have been in the mind of the apostle Paul when he wrote:

So I find it to be a law that when I want to do right, evil lies close at hand. For I delight in the law of God, in my inmost self, but I see in my members another law at war with the law of my mind and making me captive to the law of sin which dwells in my members. Wretched man that I am! Who will deliver me from this body of death? Thanks be to God through Jesus Christ our Lord! So then, I of myself serve the law of God with my mind, but with my flesh I serve the law of sin (Rom. 7:21-25)

This is one thing Paul and I have in common—the war between will and action. Knowing that Christ's greatest apostle, the man who wrote a large part of the New Testament, could write that ought to remove some of the morbid self-condemnation from which so many of us suffer.

In the darkness of the night when I awake and am sleepless, I can think of no conceivable virtue that I possess. All I can see are mistakes, errors, sins, defects of mind and heart. The self-condemnatory spirit that I encounter in the darkness is born of a legalistic religious background. We were assured, Sunday after Sunday, that we were rotten and deserved only God's severest judgment.

Compassion for Sinners

It is not judgment and condemnation that most people need, nor do they need to be shown where they have failed, how defective they are. Love is needed. Criticism degrades and generates self-hate, whereas love and compassion create a desire to be worthy of love.

I am sure there is a place for the prophetic voice to sound warnings to society concerning its evils. However, if we are to follow the example of Jesus, we should mix the proportions of compassion in a ratio of twenty to one—twenty parts compassion and love to one part condemnation. I have never known anyone to respond positively to condemnation as to understanding and love.

I have an enormous distaste for the condemnatory preacher, thundering his denunciations of all who have sinned, as though everyone who has fallen into temptation deliberately planned it.

Go through your New Testament. Pick out the times when Jesus condemned people. What do you find? Just one instance, when he excoriated the self-righteous Pharisees. It is a lengthy, bitter condemnation. Six times he cries out, "Woe to you, scribes and Pharisees, hypocrites!" He accuses them of extortion and rapacity, of tithing herbs but neglecting the weightier matters of the law, justice, mercy, and faith. He culminates the accusation with, "You serpents, you brood of vipers, how are you to escape being sentenced to hell?" (Matt. 23:13-33).

The people he condemned were the religious leaders, who considered themselves vastly superior to the rabble, whom they designated as sinners "who do not know the law." Jesus did not accuse the Pharisees of immorality. The sins for which he judged them so harshly were sins of the spirit—pride, hypocrisy, greed, and self-righteousness.

But how did he treat the people whose sins were those of the flesh? It was always with exquisite tenderness and compassion. He did not condone physical sins, but neither did he condemn. He preached the good news of forgiveness and redemption, not the bad news that they were sinners. He said, responding to John the Baptist's query as to whether he were the Messiah, "The blind receive their sight and the lame walk, lepers are cleansed and the deaf hear, and the dead are raised up, and the poor have good news preached to them" (Matt. 11:5).

When Ruth Carter Stapleton, sister of former President Carter, spent considerable time trying to bring the gospel to Larry Flynt, one of the nation's top purveyors of pornography, she was roundly criticized by some of the clergy for having anything to do with him. Surely this is a typical Pharisaical attitude which Jesus condemned so vehemently.

Jesus manifested compassion, not judgment. He healed people's physical symptoms, released them from their emotional hang-ups, and touched them where they were hurting. In some cases he forgave their sins, for the sins seemed to be the cause of their distress. In most instances he simply loved them and met their needs.

Sin is a reality. I do not discount it in the slightest, but it is the condemnatory preaching that I find so destructive. Most people do not need judgment, but compassion and understanding. I am not prepared to judge, in any human being, how will, heredity, and environment converge to bring about a sinful act. Let me illustrate.

I have a friend, a minister, whose son is a psychopathic deviate; that is, he is entirely devoid of any moral sense. He is frequently in prison, always in trouble, eternally on the run.

How would you react to a person who buys automobiles with bad checks and then leaves town; who marries a succession of women and abandons them; who leaves a string of forged checks in his wake; who steals, lies, and cheats?

Such a person is literally incapable of profiting from

experience. There is no moral sense, no internal censor, no sense of guilt or wrongdoing. He is driven by some inexplicable urge that defeats him and causes everyone in his path to suffer.

It is an easy judgment to make. Such a man should be locked up and the key thrown away, he's just no good. And the evaluation is basically sound.

What we do not know is how his genetic wiring and his environment, together with circumstances and will, combined to produce such an emotionally maladjusted individual. We dare not judge.

A majority of habitual criminals can be classified as sociopaths or psychopathic deviates, virtually incapable of profiting from experience. They continue to commit the same crimes, often leaving unmistakable clues. Larry was a case in point. After three terms in San Quentin Prison, he "graduated" from a prison Yokefellow group and was paroled to us. On his previous and last crime spree, in an unconscious effort to be apprehended, he signed his real, full name to his bad checks: Larry Napoleon Baulch. Of course, he was caught and sent up for a third term. But even a psychopathic deviate like Larry finally was won over by love and compassion. When he was released, he entered the ministry.

Just to show how hard it is to judge on the basis of reality, look at a young Catholic priest, Stephen, who took some training at our counseling center. He told of his early childhood. When he was four, his father had a severe heart attack. The mother said, "I want you to be a good boy now, because Daddy's very sick." So, in an all-out effort to be a good boy he became quiet, and very "good," to keep Daddy alive. Since children are good observers but poor interpreters, the boy was consciously good, and unconsciously determined to be absolutely perfect. He said to me, "I'm twenty-eight years old, and I've spent twenty-four of those years trying diligently to be good. I wonder if I entered the priesthood in an effort to achieve supreme goodness."

I said, "Perhaps all of us have mixed motives in some degree; but if God had to wait for perfectly pure motives, he would certainly be shorthanded." He smiled and said, "I can accept that." Larry, the psychopathic deviate, seemed driven by some inner compulsion to destroy himself by his antisocial acts; Stephen, driven by an unconscious obsession with "goodness" ended up in the priesthood. How can one explain such an anomaly?

Sin and Belief

Hidden sin and guilt often determine what we believe. A man visited me once ostensibly to discuss some of his religious perplexities. He said that he had studied Zen Buddhism, the Muslim faith, Confucianism, New Thought, Spiritialism, Pyramidism, Anglo-Israelism, and astrology, trying to discover the one true faith.

I said, "I expect that in your search you found many great truths. I notice, however, that you did not mention having studied Christianity. I suppose you have read the Bible as diligently as you have the Koran, for instance."

"No," he said, "actually I just never got around to reading the Bible, but I think I have a pretty good idea of what it's all about."

Before the hour was up I discovered that he had no

genuine interest in discovering the reality of God. He had not the slightest intention of bringing his will into harmony with any mind greater than his own. His personal life needed cleaning up, so he could not accept any religion which required the surrender of his personal pride and the abandonment of his immorality.

A giant of a man came to me for counseling. John, as I'll call him, had an enormous anxiety neurosis, so severe that at times he was unable to function on the job, or even to take care of his own personal affairs. He had become a Christian several years before, and for a time he functioned beautifully, teaching a Sunday school class and witnessing in addition to doing well in his own personal life. Then suddenly, for no apparent reason, he was seized with an uncontrollable anxiety. He had spent considerable time and money seeing a psychologist without obtaining relief.

He assured me that he had had a good childhood, a statement that I am usually prepared neither to accept nor reject. In his Primal Integration sessions, during which he was taken back to relive traumatic events of his early life, it was discovered that he had had an unbelievably bad childhood. He relived those events with as much intensity as he did during the original event—with tears and anger. He discharged, in a number of sessions, an enormous amount of child-hood pain and hurts. However, he still experienced an excessive amount of anxiety for which we were unable to account. I questioned him about his diet and discovered that it was atrocious. He was put on a proper diet. He improved considerably, but something was wrong. We had his mineral balance checked and found that his lifelong faulty eating habits had given him a severe imbalance. He improved in the next few weeks, but his excessive anxiety still persisted.

In one Primal session I asked him about guilt feelings. He told me that all of his sins had been confessed and forgiven when he became a Christian. However, I took him on a guided tour of his entire adult life, and at one point where he relived some of his army experience, he began to unload, with deep intensity, a mountain of guilt. He relived every rotten thing he had ever done. Then he confessed it, with intense feeling, asking God's forgiveness. The session lasted two hours.

Now, at long last, his enormous anxiety neurosis was gone. He told me later, "I thought I had confessed all that stuff, and I had, but it must not have been a very deep confession. That session upstairs on the mat was really deep, wasn't it? That's one of the important things I needed all along, together with going back over my childhood and dumping all the fear and hurt and anger I had pent up inside me."

A year later he was still functioning beautifully on the job and teaching a Bible class, even taking the pulpit on Layman's Sunday. After all the hurt, grief, and guilt were totally cleaned out, he not only was rid of his neurosis, but he also began to lose weight without effort. The last time I saw him, more than a year after our last session, he had lost forty-nine pounds and had a few more pounds to lose. No man could have been happier.

It would have been simplistic to say to such a man, "All you need to do is to get right with God. Confess your sins and receive Christ as your Savior." He had done that to the best of his ability. Or to say, "Since you are suffering from a severe anxiety neurosis, you should talk it out with a psychiatrist." He had tried that, too. Condemnation and simplistic answers were not the solution. Talk therapy does not always suffice for deeply buried hurts and guilt.

Where did sin—this widespread contamination that has infected us all—come from? We learn from the Bible that Lucifer, son of the morning, was the most beautiful and perfect angel in heaven. The angels, originally created to serve and glorify God, rebelled against God. Lucifer (Satan) led the rebellion. He wanted to rule in the place of God. He said, "I will exalt my throne above the stars of God; and I will sit upon the mount of congregation, . . . I will ascend above the heights of the clouds; I will make myself like the Most High" (Isa. 14:13-14 ASV). Notice the repetitious use of the personal pronoun: "I . . . I . . . I . . . I."

He was guilty of pride—one of the seven deadly sins. Pride has always been believed to be one of the greatest of sins. Lucifer wanted to be like God, to have power equal to or greater than that of God. It was at this point that the Bible describes him tempting Adam and Eve—getting them to disobey God out of pride.

I am often asked if I believe in the devil. My response is that if there isn't a devil, someone is certainly doing his work for him. Whether or not he is a distinct personality isn't important. Jesus spoke of him as if he were a personality, whether figuratively or literally may be open to debate. I am personally convinced on the authority of the Bible that he exists, in opposition to God.

This doesn't mean that "the devil made me do it," when I sin. I cannot lay all the blame on him. I have

[35]

enough inherent tendency toward evil within me so
that I don't require the assistance of some diabolical
agency. The Genesis story is an attempt to explain the
origin of that tendency.

What Is Sin?

Sin can be defined in a hundred ways, each
definition containing some truth. For the sake of
brevity, let me say that sin is trying to pursue
incompatible moral goals. It is willing anything that
is less than perfect. It is being a confirmed materialist.
It is pride, envy, greed, grudge-bearing, malice,
dishonesty.

So it is not only the sins of the flesh, destructive as
they are; it is vastly more than that. Sin is, at its core,
failure to want the whole will of God, failure to love,
and much more.

I suppose I could put it all in a nutshell and say that
sin is anything short of perfection. That is why Paul
said, "All have sinned and fall short of the glory of
God."

Sin is not only the "bad" things we do, or our failure
to do "good" things. Sin is envy of those who have
what we desire. Sin is pride that springs out of our
basic sense of inferiority. Sin is pretending to be
different than we are and holding up this mask of
pretense so long that we finally do not know which is
the real self and which is the phony.

Sin is passing judgment without having all the facts.
Sin is failure to forgive, and, above all, failure to show
compassion. Jesus "looked around at them with
anger, grieved at their hardness of heart" (Mark 3:5).
They lacked compassion.

Sin is refusal to do what I know I ought to do, granted that I am capable. "Whoever knows what is right to do and fails to do it, for him it is sin" (James 4:17).

Persons can be morally upright citizens, peacefully watching television, yet be living in sin in the sight of God, if at that moment they know inwardly that they should be doing something else.

Sin is offering frantic service to God as a substitute for communion with him; for, more than he wants our service, he desires our love and fellowship. Sin is spiritual sloth, wanting God's blessings but unwilling to place ourselves at his disposal. Sin is essentially what we are, not what we do.

Above all, sin is failure to love God, failure to love one's neighbor, and failure to love oneself properly. For "He who does not love does not know God; for God is love" (I John 4:8).

What should we do about sin? Until recently the Roman Catholic Church specified confession to a priest. Now it has made a significant change in its conduct of the confessional. The darkened confessional box, the guilty whispering sins to a hidden priest, and the solemnly prescribed penance of a set number of prayers have given way to a new procedure.

Many dioceses have now instituted well-lighted, cheerful "reconciliation rooms," where emphasis is on forgiveness rather than guilt. The sacrament of confession begins with a warm greeting from the priest, then moves on to a scripture reading, confession, discussion of sins and suggested ways of dealing with them. The priest's role is changing from that of judge to one of sensitive healing.

[37]

The change has been made in response to an alarming 20 percent decrease in the number of people who go to confession. This would appear to be a long step in the right direction. The practice of whispering one's sins into the ear of a listening priest, then receiving a penalty (doing penance) seems outmoded, if not downright futile. What is the point of confessing symptomatic sins over and over and saying a set number of "Our Fathers" or "Hail Marys" as penance, when the original cause of the defect is never brought to light? Regardless of one's religious orientation, the confessing, for instance, of alcoholism, or promiscuous sexual behavior, is simply confessing symptomatic behavior without discovering the source of the problem. A person does not become an alcoholic from choice or become sexually promiscuous out of the desire to lead an immoral life.

The problem drinker is trying to tranquilize his nameless anxiety; he needs a drink in order to face life, because he lacks inner resources. The sexually promiscuous individual is usually sexualizing his or her anxiety—searching for Daddy, or Mother, for a warm, loving response.

Confession is important. In fact we are told to confess our sins to God and to one another. However, long ago I ceased to confess my individual sins and began to search inwardly for the impaired emotions out of which the defective behavior grew. It is no use confessing an angry outburst. Why am I an angry person inwardly? It is fruitless to confess a lie unless one is willing to look within and discover the basic reason for lying. It is not the sin but the sinner who needs to be confessed. Rather a person should say:

"Lord, I am often angry; I hold grudges; I am not always truthful; I do not forgive others in every instance; and there are times when I am not totally honest. I see within myself a great deal of hate. I am not a loving person. I see that these are only symptoms of some basic malfunction within me, some spiritual and emotional immaturity which takes these forms. I confess my spiritual need, my emotional hang-ups. I will probably be this way for a long time to come unless I receive divine help in finding out why I act as I do. Help me discover why I am the impaired person I perceive myself as being. Help me to want your will."

It is not always easy to say with all honesty, "I want the whole will of God." Sometimes we fear that to desire God's whole will might cause us to end up as missionaries in the New Hebrides, make us give up some of our pleasures, or fight a spiritual battle we are afraid of losing.

If you have difficult in this area, I suggest a formula which I have used with gratifying success. Simply say slowly and thoughtfully, five to ten times a day in those little chinks of time, "I *want* to want the whole will of God!" Keep it up for ninety days. Each time you make this affirmation you are taking one more step toward the day when you say, as you ultimately will, "No, I don't want to want the will of God, I *want* his whole will!" Let nothing deter you. It is a glorious adventure and can bring you great peace. You may find you need to keep this up for longer than ninety days, for humans are very leaky vessels. But what a gratifying victory when you can say, "I *do* want the whole will of God in every area of my life."

Can Evil Be Explained?

No one has ever satisfactorily explained that triumvirate of evil: sin, suffering, and sorrow. Theologians struggle mightily and propound their theories, but a component is missing. If five factors are needed to solve a problem and you have only four, you will never solve it. Something is missing.

How, for instance, would you endeavor to explain this: a violent hurricane roared down on Santo Domingo, with gales of ninety to a hundred miles an hour. Four hundred and eighty people fled their homes and gathered in a church for safety. A flooded river changed its course and leveled the church, drowning four hundred people who had been praying for deliverance.

Albert Camus speaks of "the benevolent indifference of nature," but I think that those sufferers would not use the word benevolent. Nature does seem basically benevolent, but at times it can be malevolent, brutal, as well as indifferent.

I recall spending an hour or so with a heartbroken widow at a seminar I was conducting. Her story was this: her husband's niece had dropped by their home one evening in a lovely new car and had invited her uncle to take a ride around the block to try it out. They went for a short ride, and a block away from home they were struck by a hit-and-run driver. The uncle was killed instantly.

How can one explain that to a widow? No one can say anything to lift the burden of grief and anger from such a person. Again we find the inexplicable corporate guilt of society intruding into a home and destroying it.

An associate of mine, a former pastor, told me of a

friend of his who had occasional epileptic seizures. He had a wife and three small children. On one occasion when he was alone, he had a seizure and fell into a shallow pool of water and drowned. How can we make sense of that?

The three-year-old granddaughter of friends was left in the care of a sister for a brief time. While the older child was preoccupied for a few moments, the three-year-old wandered into the backyard, fell into the swimming pool, and drowned. What does one say to the distraught parents?

A letter from a woman tells of her tragic situation. She has had three bad marriages. The first husband was an alcoholic who beat her and abused their three children. Her second husband couldn't hold a job and was verbally and physically abusive. He loafed at home while she worked to support the family. The third husband was also an alcoholic who beat her and the children. She is now divorced, with three children to support.

What genetic tendencies, or environmental factors, predisposed her to marry three such men? Or was it rather a sequence of circumstances, together with desperation, that led her to make those choices? Here we are confronted with a situation difficult to solve. Would you care to advise her? Or judge her? Small wonder that Jesus, who "knew what was in man" cautioned us not to judge, lest we be judged.

In Nikos Kazantzakis' *Zorba the Greek*, after the young widow has been killed by an angry, lusting mob of men, Zorba asks his young English employer, "What do all your books tell us about why people have to die?" The Englishman answers, "They tell us about the agony of men who can't answer questions like yours."

There is no simple explanation for the ongoing, mounting evils of modern society, nor for the moral and spiritual failures we humans experience. One of America's outstanding preachers said that he had stopped trying to explain human suffering. He says he has "abandoned all the standard religious ways of justifying God's apparently harmful ways to man, of answering the eternal question, 'Why did this happen if God is love?' " His conclusion is, "I believe the Christian gospel, not because it offers the best explanation of human suffering, but because it gives the strength we need to win through."

Can There Be Meaning to Suffering?

We know that God does not bring disaster or sorrow into our lives in order to teach us a lesson or to punish us. The Bible tells us that "in everything God works for good with those who love him, who are called according to his purpose" (Rom. 8:28). This is beautifully illustrated in the life of Joni Eareckson who was pretty, popular, and the "Most Athletic Girl" in her high school. After she broke her neck in a diving accident, she was forced to spend her life in a wheelchair, paralyzed from the neck down. Joni went through periods of deep despair, but after

years of tough rehabilitation, she taught herself to draw and paint, holding a pen or a brush between her teeth. Then came speaking tours and writing, in which she uses her own faith to encourage the despairing and disabled. Last year she organized a national "ministry to those who suffer" called Joni and Friends. . . . It offers both spiritual and practical advice to as many as 2,000 letter writers each week. . . .

In the evangelistic side of her work, Eareckson faces head-on the universal problem that is central to her life and as old as the *Book of Job:* If a loving God exists, why do the good and the apparently innocent suffer? After she wrote her autobiography *Joni* (1976), 120,000 letters poured in, mostly with variations on the question. . . . She also wrote a 1978 book on the issue, called *A Step Further* (Zondervan; $6.95). It is a plain-spoken version of points often made by Christian writers: for example, "If God's mind was small enough for me to understand, he wouldn't be God." . . .

Eventually she concluded . . . that man cannot understand the whys and ways of God regarding pain, but that knowledge of Christ's life and suffering makes pain endurable. "The Bible underscored that I didn't have to hold on to the value that society placed on my life," she says. "Sometimes I can't stand being in a wheelchair, but then God's grace takes over. Even in my handicap, God has a plan and purpose for my life." (*Time,* December 29, 1980)

Hers is a magnificent testimony to the power of faith in a God we cannot understand, but one we see mirrored in Christ.

3

What Is the Will of God for You?

Free will is God's do-it-yourself kit.

—*Larry Eisenberg*

You live only once, but once is enough if you play it right.

—*Fred Allen*

A religion small enough for our understanding would not be large enough for our needs.

—*Arthur Balfour*

We were riding from Jerusalem to Bethlehem with Musa, our friend, guide, and driver. He is a Palestinian Christian whom I had known for twenty-five years. He has driven us around the Holy Land on several previous trips.

Musa had nine children, and had just announced the imminent arrival of a tenth. Knowing something of his rather tight financial situation I said, "Musa, I would like to make you a gift. When I return to the United States, I will send you a year's supply of birth control pills."

Musa said, thoughtfully but firmly, "Thank you,

Dr. Osborne, I appreciate the offer, but I do not feel we should reject what God sends."

I said, "Musa, I have a message for you from God. It is this: God has nothing to do with it. It is entirely up to you and your wife."

"What do you mean? God is in charge of this world, isn't he?"

"No, my friend, we are. God's first gift to Adam and Eve was life. The second was free will. He turned it all over to them—and to us."

"Ah, but he also said, 'Be fruitful and multiply.' "

"True, but to make a fruit tree fruitful you have to prune it back every year. Overpopulation in India, for instance, is a good example of bad planning. The country can never prosper until the people practice birth control."

But Musa was unconvinced. He continued to believe that God is in charge and, in common with millions of others, ascribes all that happens to the intentional will of God, believing that there is no way people can control their own destiny.

Enshallah is a word the Muslims employ frequently. It means literally, "the will of God," or, "if God wills it," but it is used in the sense of "nothing can be done about it." This is a very handy though erroneous religious attitude. It enables the poor to be philosophical about poverty—"*Enshallah*. It is the will of God." And it absolves the wealthy of any responsibility for the poor.

Bill Moyers, former special assistant to President Lyndon Johnson, once wrote:

I was in London with an official of the Saudi Arabian government, preparing to interview him on television, when . . . my associate brought word that King Faisal had been murdered. The man slumped against a table and shook his head in disbelief. . . .

The man grimaced and continued to shake his head in a slow roll of grief. Finally, he said: "I loved him. He was my King and friend, and I loved him." . . .

His eyes were moist when he spoke again: "It was God's will. It had to be God's will."

"I stopped believing a long time ago in a God who wills murder," I said. "These things are governed by insanity, or blind passion, not Providence."

He turned and put both hands on my shoulders. "Today is the birthday of Muhammad," he said. "God has always used Faisal and it is God who has willed this. Only God could find in this awful thing a purpose to justify it. If I could not believe that, I would myself die. And you—you must not stop believing in a purposeful God. . . .

"You must believe it, too. It is all we have, my friend—our belief in the will of God. Do not give it up." (*Newsweek*, April 7, 1975)

Many Christians have a similar view. The term "will of God" is often misused to cover all that happens. We are told to be "resigned to God's will," when there is a sudden catastrophe. Insurance people, for instance, apply the term "act of God" to a natural disaster, such as a flood or a hurricane—a gross misapplication of the term.

It was not God who willed the death of six million Jews; it was Hitler. It was not God who killed an estimated thirty million Chinese, it was Mao Tse-tung; it was not God who exterminated eighty-five thousand people at Hiroshima, it was an atomic bomb manufactured in the U.S. An equal number died in Berlin in the final days of that war. God willed none of that. These horrors were committed by humans. God permitted but did not cause them.

A young man who came for intensive counseling described in grim detail the scene when his father was killed. He was six years old at the time. In an effort to comfort him, a relative said, "God took your Daddy; he's with Jesus now." It was poor comfort. The young man said, "That meant to me that God was a murderer, and for many years I had a severe headache whenever I went to church. I never knew why until I relived that childhood scene in a Primal Integration session."

I explained that God does not kill a little boy's daddy. It is not God's intentional will that a boy should lose his father or that a father should lose his child.

What Is God's Will?

What do I mean by God's intentional will? Several years ago Leslie D. Weatherhead wrote a book entitled *The Will of God* in which he discussed three aspects of God's will, three ways in which God is involved in our lives. They are (1) his *intentional* will, (2) his *circumstantial* will, and (3) his *ultimate* will.

It was surely not God's intent that Jesus should be crucified. Yes, his death had been prophesied, but prophecy means foretelling and does not imply that the act has been foreordained. Jesus, looking out over Jerusalem, prophesied the forthcoming destruction of the city and wept as he contemplated that fact. His prophecy was simply the announcing of a forthcoming event. He neither willed it nor caused it.

God's intention was surely that people would hear

and obey Jesus, not kill him. Someone may respond to that statement by saying, "Without Jesus' death there could have been no salvation. It was his atoning death that saves us."

But God did not change when Jesus died. *Jesus' sacrificial death was the living out, the demonstration, of what had always been true about the nature of God.* Forgiveness did not begin with the death of Jesus. Divine pardon was freely offered in the Old Testament. God did not extend loving compassion for the first time in response to his son's death. No, God did not intend the death of his son, though prophets *foresaw* and foretold the event.

That brings us to the second aspect of God's will: his circumstantial will.

Under the circumstances of the trial of Jesus, and his condemnation to death by the authorities at the instigation of the Jewish leaders, what happened becomes the *circumstantial* will of God. God operates now within the circumstances which were the result of evil.

Let me illustrate: I have referred to a young man named Larry, who spent three terms in San Quentin Prison. He was a forger, and such people, prison authorities tell me, are among the most difficult to rehabilitate. In prison, Larry joined a Yokefellow group led by the chaplain who used material I had provided. I met Larry in the prison chapel a year after he joined the group.

Sometime later he was granted parole on the condition that he have the promise of a job. I couldn't find a job for an ex-convict who had never done an honest day's work in his life, but believing in his sincerity, I created a temporary job for him as assistant custodian. Before the year was out, Larry was enrolled in a theological seminary, studying for the ministry. When he completed the course, he began to work with prisoners, helping, among other things, to establish two halfway houses. He died just a few years ago, after laboring wonderfully in his chosen field, the rehabilitation of ex-prisoners.

Obviously it was not God's will for Larry to become a criminal and be sentenced to prison, but while there he came under the benevolent influence of a fine chaplain and a Yokefellow group. God worked *under the circumstances.*

Larry once asked me, thoughtfully, "How do you explain the difference between free will and fate?" I said, "I'm not sure I have all the answers, Larry, but the best way I can put it is this: in a card game *fate* is the hand you are given; *free will* is the way you play it."

He had been dealt a bad hand, environmentally; he had had a rejecting father and an unloving mother. His first theft was when he was a boy. He entered the home of his best friend when no one was there, despite the fact that his friend's father was chief of police, and stole some items. He asked me one day, "Why did I do such a stupid thing?"

"My best guess," I said, "is that you were envious of your friend's relationship with his father."

"Oh, yes, I often envied him. His father was a great person."

"Then you were stealing something from the father, a symbolic substitute for the loving father you longed for and could not have. Much childhood stealing is just that—taking some object, or money, as a substitute for love. It explains but does not justify your first criminal act."

So, God had been at work redemptively in Larry's life under the *circumstances* of his imprisonment, which was not a part of God's *intentional* will.

The life and teachings of Jesus make it clear that the perfect will of God for his children is love, joy, peace, and total fulfillment. We have seen how, under his circumstantial will, a warped society damages us and renders us less than whole persons.

So, God's intentional will has temporarily been thwarted by evil. Does that mean that a depraved humankind will forever prove stronger than God? Is Satan stronger than God? Can God be defeated?

The Bible is very clear on this point. In scores of passages, in both the Old and New Testaments, we are assured of the ultimate triumph of God. The Revelation speaks of the day when "The kingdom of this world now belongs to our Lord, and to his Christ; and he shall reign forever and ever" (Rev. 11:15 TLB). The present tense is used because John is reporting his vision of the end of the age when Christ returns to reign in power.

We are taught to pray for this in the Lord's Prayer, "Thy kingdom come, / Thy will be done / On earth as it is in heaven" (Matt. 6:10). Jesus here makes it clear that there will be a time when God's ultimate will is to be done on earth, just as it is in heaven, where his perfect, glorious will prevails.

God cannot be defeated. There will be a day when, as the Bible tells us in figurative language, Satan shall be bound for a thousand years. I don't pretend to understand perfectly all the prophecies. But the implication is clear; the powers of evil will be shackled at the edict of God:

[50]

Then I saw an angel coming down from heaven, holding in his hand the key of the bottomless pit and a great chain. And he seized the dragon, that ancient serpent, who is the Devil and Satan, and bound him for a thousand years, and threw him into the pit, and shut it and sealed it over him, that he should deceive the nations no more, till the thousand years were ended. After that he must be loosed for a little while. (Rev. 20:1-3)

It would be fruitless, of course, to attempt to interpret these symbols literally; but the import is quite clear: Satan, whoever he is or whatever he represents, is to be held in check for a thousand years. For some reason not explained, he is then released for a brief period.

We know how the story ends. The prophets unite in proclaiming the day when Christ shall reign supreme and God's will shall be done on earth. This is his ultimate will.

How Do We Experience the Will of God?

Not everyone is going to experience God's *intentional* will for fulfillment and happiness. For instance, since women live eight to nine years longer than men on the average, women outnumber men. Some of them will never marry, probably due to the shortage of men. This is not the intentional will of God, but the result of the corporate guilt of society—the stress and wars which take their toll of men. The net result is that some women will never know the fulfillment of bearing and nurturing children.

I have been told that prior to World War II it was the practice in hospitals to require lengthy bed care for patients following both major surgery and childbirth.

During the war when London was being bombed nightly, it was necessary to get patients down to the bomb shelter when the air raid sirens sounded. To the surprise of physicians, people who were gotten up out of bed soon after an operation recovered much faster than those who were allowed to remain in bed without exercise. This discovery appears to be one of many significant benefits derived from the war.

Does this mean that "God uses war to provide benefits for society," as one person explained it? Hardly. God does not intend inconceivable human suffering and the death of millions so that a bit of progress may be made by society. He *permits* war, sin, suffering, and sorrow, because it is compatible with the free will with which he has endowed us. He allowed the Dark Ages to blanket Europe for a thousand years, the black plague to kill millions of people, the fire of London to destroy most of the city. But the fact that good sometimes comes out of evil does not in any sense imply that God intentionally wills evil. God can *use* our suffering, but he does not intend it.

We know from the life and example of Jesus that sickness and suffering are not a part of God's purpose. We read that "many followed him, and he healed them all" (Matt. 12:15). Jesus did not say to any, "Yours is a terminal case," and turn them away; he healed all of them. From this we draw the logical conclusion that God wills the health and well-being of everyone. He does not send sickness so that we may learn some lesson.

I recall hearing someone tell about a non-Christian family whose teen-age daughter had been killed in an accident. The pastor who conducted the funeral ministered to the family in their grief, and eventually the family made a profession of faith and united with the church. My informant said, "Isn't it wonderful the way God planned it all?" I said, "No, God didn't plan the death of the young woman. He did use the parents' grief to bring about something creative, but God does not kill children to get their parents' attention."

Let us take the phrase that the apostle Paul used in his address at Athens: " 'In him we live and move and have our being' " (Acts 17:28). Instead of viewing God as a distant deity out in space, who observes us much as a person sitting on a porch might view the passerby, or who manipulates events from a distance, let us suppose that we are, as Paul says, "in" him—entities living within God—like cells in a body. Imagine for a moment that he knows what is happening to us because he feels within himself our sorrows and our pleasures and suffers or rejoices with us.

You and I are very important to him, being a part of him. This concept changes him from a distant deity, observing us without really experiencing our pain and our pleasure, to a God who is present with us, "Closer than hands and feet," to use Tennyson's phrase. In no other way would Paul's affirmation make any real sense.

If this is true, then God loves us and wills our best to the same degree that he loves himself. He feels all that we experience, our pain, our joy, our victories, and our defeats.

No one understands fully why God permits evil. But I am confident that we can trust him. Paul says, "Godly grief produces a repentance that leads to salvation and brings no regret, but worldly grief produces death" (II Cor. 7:10). Moffatt's translation refers to "the pain God is allowed to guide" and alludes to the fact that the pagans waste their pain.

Thus, though God does not intend our pain—which I have suggested that he feels—it can be used to our advantage in stimulating our growth. I find that I pray ever so much more earnestly when I am faced with a crisis. I feel his care and concern much more keenly; I am closer to him when I am hurting. I wish it were otherwise, that I could love and desire him as intensely when all is going well. Unfortunately, we humans are not equipped to have it that way. So, if all is well with you, be grateful; but if there are sorrows, thank him—"in everything give thanks"!

Where Do Heredity, Environment, and Will Converge?

The story of Norma Zimmer (*Norma*, Tyndale House Publishers, 1976), the lovely blond soloist on the Lawrence Welk show, is both tragic and thrilling.

She was the daughter of alcoholic parents. The family lived for a time in a two-room tar-paper shack with no indoor plumbing and no running water. Her father was a hostile person, angry most of the time, though her mother was much more accepting. At times Norma wore cardboard shoes. Her parents earned a living for a while as itinerant berry pickers.

Norma was determined to make something of herself and decided to become a singer. When she sang her first solo in church, her parents staggered down the aisle drunk.

Understandably, she was a timid, self-effacing young woman, having come from such a background.

Her self-image was very weak, yet buoyed by some indefinable strength, she kept struggling to reach her goal. Along the way she became an ardent Christian. Now she had additional resources, the assurance that with prayer and determination, and some talent, she could make it.

Eventually she landed a spot on the Lawrence Welk show, but it was not a sudden rags to riches leap. It involved struggle and heartache and disappointment, yet, she made it. She is a gentle, loving, deeply sincere Christian performer.

Psychologists are uncertain as to whether environment or heredity play the major role in one's development. Perhaps it is different in some degree with each person. There appeared to be no blueprint for Norma's life, no easily discovered slot into which she could fit easily and naturally. There was a vast deal of uncertainty and struggle involved. Struggle is an important part of life. Just as a plane takes off into the wind, a human being often does best facing the odds, drawing from some hidden resources deep within sufficient strength to succeed. The halfhearted fall by the wayside, but those with singleness of purpose, determination, and the certainty that God wills their best are far more likely to reach their goals.

Who Is in Control?

Let me go back now to the idea of God's control with which we began this chapter. Frequently we hear admonitions from the pulpit to "let God control your life." This is very bad theology. God will not control anyone's life. He offers to guide, but he will not control.

A highly intelligent young man who detested his job told me that he wanted to find God's blueprint for his life.

"There isn't one," I replied. "That's a misconception." He was astounded. "But I always thought that to let God control your life meant that he would reveal his blueprint for you. Surely he has a plan for us."

"Not really," I said. "Jesus gave us some basic principles, but he left the details up to us. He tells us what our attitudes are to be, how to relate to God and man, but offers no blueprint for our lives."

My young friend was very depressed. "Here I've been searching for God's plan all my life."

"Where has it gotten you?"

"Nowhere, really; just locked into a job I hate."

I told him to be open to divine guidance. In a half-hearted way he prayed for guidance, without positive results. Then ten years later, he decided to go back to church. He and his wife rededicated their lives, started a program of daily meditation, joined a Bible study class, and began attending church regularly. Now, for the first time, he is genuinely, passionately seeking the guidance of God.

At last he found the inner peace he had sought for so long. He went from a halfhearted commitment to seek divine guidance to an all-out commitment of *himself.* God's guidance was available to him, no matter what kind of job he held, or where he lived, under any set of circumstances, but he had not sought God with all his heart. He had wanted guidance without committing himself.

God, in a sense, is in the same situation as a parent whose son or daughter has just gotten a driver's license. In our state the age is sixteen. Most young people this age feel that they are abundantly endowed with wisdom.

So, you turn the car keys over to the youngster and go to your room and pray. That happens in heaven, for us. We read that "the Holy Spirit prays for us with such feeling that it cannot be expressed in words" (Rom. 8:26 TLB). The Holy Spirit will not control us, but he will pray for us. I find that very comforting.

I could freely prophesy, after observing his driving habits, that our son, just starting to drive, would have an accident before too long. In no way could he avoid it, with his basic tendencies. So I warned him of the consequences of some of his faulty driving habits and told him I was going to pray that when the accident occurred he wouldn't hurt himself or anyone else. Within a month it happened. Two cars were wrecked, but no one was hurt. He still had one serious driving fault, of which I warned him. Then I prayed again that no one would be injured. There was another accident, but no injuries.

Henceforth he drove with infinite care. There is, for most of us, no teacher as effective as experience.

I had no desire to control my son. How do you control a sixteen-year-old person, or anyone for that matter, without making a robot out of him? I wanted only his best. And that is precisely what God wills for us.

What Is the Will of God for You?

As I have already stated, there is, in my opinion, no divine blueprint for your life rolled up and stuck in some heavenly pigeonhole. You are in the same position as the pilot of a small plane; you are flying solo. You know the rules and regulations; you choose your own destination from any one of several thousand landing fields. *You are in charge.*

But there are resources available to you. The control tower can give you your bearings, guide you in to a safe landing, warn of dangers, give you information about impending storms. The man in the control tower does not determine your destination. You are free to go and come at will, to choose your own course. But if you keep in touch with the control tower, you can be spared a great deal of anxiety and uncertainty and perhaps a crash. That man in the tower is as concerned about you as about any other pilot up there, including the pilot of a 747. All of his resources are available to you.

The air traffic controller will not control you or impose his will on you. Nor will God control you, but he does long to guide you lovingly, gently.

The wife of the young man who had been locked into a detested job told me, when her husband finally found his niche and began for the first time to succeed in every area of life: "We were Christians, but didn't work at it. We drank too much, trying to tranquilize our anxiety; but when we started going to church, and got into that Bible study class, and had daily meditation, and really sought God's will in every area of our lives, good things began to happen. We had begun seeking not just his guidance, but him."

That, in short, is what makes the big difference.

4

Prayer—Fact, Fallacy, or Magic?

Prayer is the soul's sincere desire,
Uttered or unexpressed.

—*James Montgomery*

During World War II I read various accounts, each slightly different, concerning a soldier whose life had been saved when an enemy bullet lodged in a New Testament he was carrying in his left breast pocket.

I heard the same story with variations during the Korean war. One account had the infantryman carrying an entire Bible in his breast pocket. The bullet in this case allegedly penetrated the pages up to the ninety-first Psalm and pointed directly to the verse which read: "A thousand may fall at your side, / ten thousand at your right hand; / but it shall not come near you" (Ps. 91:7).

The story lives on in other forms, such as this one from a San Mateo, California, newspaper, concerning a soldier in Vietnam whose life was saved in a similar fashion. "A deck of playing cards sent from San Mateo, California, saved the life of an embattled soldier in Vietnam." The account continued: "The cards were part of a package sent to the Third Brigade of the Fourth Infantry Division by Operation Home-front." If such accounts are to be believed, then a deck of playing cards are as effective in stopping bullets as a New Testament.

Where do naïveté and magic end, and fact and faith begin?

The single survivor of a plane crash writes ecstatically of the way in which his prayers were answered. One wonders why he was singled out to live when more than a hundred others died.

Thousands of early Christians died of torture at the hands of the Romans. An untold number of Christians, accused of heresy, died during the Inquisition. What happened to their prayers?

These victims were not spared, nor were number-less missionaries who have died in accidents and at the hand of those to whom they were sent. Their prayers for deliverance were not answered. Why? Does prayer work? What is the use of having faith?

Should We Take Jesus Literally?

Jesus made some very all-inclusive statements about faith and prayer which seem to imply that we should be able to get anything we ask for. Take these, for example:

"If you have faith and never doubt, . . . if you say to this mountain, 'Be taken up and cast into the sea,' it will be done. And whatever you ask in prayer, you will receive, if you have faith" (Matt. 21:21-22).

"Whatever you ask in my name, I will do it, that the Father may be glorified in the Son; if you ask anything in my name, I will do it" (John 14:13-14).

"Again, I tell you that if two of you on earth agree

about anything you ask for, it will be done for you by my Father in heaven" (Matt. 18:19 NIV).

There are numerous other promises, just as explicit. We must, in all honesty, deal with these. Since so many earnest prayers are not granted, there must be an answer other than the guilt-inducing, "You just don't have enough faith."

Some of Jesus' statements about prayer cannot be taken literally, as millions of faithful Christians can testify. You cannot just ask for anything you want and get it. The apostle Paul asked three times that his thorn in the flesh—whatever it was—be removed. The answer he finally received was, "My grace is sufficient for you" (II Cor. 12:9). This does not seem to be an altogether satisfying response for a man who, as has been speculated, suffered from a disfiguring eye disease, or some other physical defect which rendered him less than attractive. He even reports that the members of the church at Corinth spoke disparagingly of his personality. This physical defect would have impaired his preaching, because in the same verse he quotes them as saying that "You have never heard a worse preacher" (II Cor. 10:10 TLB).

Surely, if there was ever a time for a mountainous problem to be removed, this was it. Yet Paul remained handicapped.

What is the answer? Let's consider some of the possibilities.

Jesus was misquoted. This seems very unlikely. The numerous Gospel accounts of his utterances on the subject of prayer are quite explicit.

Jesus directed these promises exclusively to his twelve disciples—in each case he was speaking directly to them. It is not explicitly stated, however, nor even implied, that the promises were intended only for them. It would have to be an inference, based on the facts that he was not talking to a crowd of people, hence presumably not to us, and that the disciples were a specially chosen group. Few Christians accept this explanation.

Something is missing from the statement. That is, we can consider the possibility that Jesus' statements were not always quoted in their entirety. For instance, one of his teachings on the subject contains a powerful condition: "I am the vine, you are the branches. He who abides in me, and I in him, he it is that bears much fruit. . . . *If you abide in me, and my words abide in you,* ask whatever you will and it shall be done for you" (John 15:5-7, italics added).

The vine and branches analogy implies maintaining an intensely close relationship with Jesus. It suggests that one would need to be in more or less constant communion with him, and totally obedient, with the same kind of oneness Jesus had with the Father.

Jesus Lays Down Conditions

That puts an entirely different light on prayer, doesn't it? Instead of a blank check, here are some very difficult conditions. (Read John 14, 15, and 16, as well as John 10:1-17.) Let's review them.

First, Jesus says that we must be related to him in the same manner as the branch that has a living, growing relationship with the vine. This suggests a very, very *intimate relationship* with him.

Second, we are to *obey his commands.* This implies more than a set of intellectual beliefs about Jesus. We are called to obey him implicitly, unconditionally.

Reread his teachings and see how many of his commands you aren't now obeying. (Are you getting a little discouraged?)

Third, he demands that we *love one another as much as he loves us.* (Now it's getting still more difficult, isn't it?) He loved the Twelve, and he loves us, with unconditional, redemptive love. And we poor faulty humans are called to love one another as much as *that!*

Fourth, he defines the depth of this kind of love we are to manifest for one another. We must be *willing to lay down our lives* for one another; not just for our loved ones and close friends, but for any of the Christian fellowship—anywhere! (He keeps laying it on us, doesn't he?)

Fifth, he explains it still further by saying that he regards the Twelve no longer as servants but as *friends.* Then he elaborates: those who obey him are his friends, and *they* are the ones who can ask what they will!

This kind of relationship which Jesus asks of us is dealt with in Thomas Kelly's little classic, *Testament of Devotion.* Kelly develops the idea that while carrying out our daily tasks we should be more or less in constant communion with Christ. In a kind of simultaneity, we may be engaged in a conversation, while with another portion of the mind, we remain in nonverbal communion with Christ.

This, of course, is a far cry from the "magic" concept of prayer, in which one asks and receives whatever he wants.

To sum up, *all of Jesus' statements about prayer need to be taken together.* The seeming blank check, "If you ask anything in my name, I will do it," must be modified by all his other statements.

Characteristics of Answered Prayer

My own experience with answered prayer provides me with some disquieting, yet hopeful, observations. They are disquieting because they do not involve magical "ask and get" results; gratifying because they validate a basic assumption about prayer, which is: God does answer prayer, but there are certain inescapable conditions that seem to be characteristic of answered prayer.

Prayer must be intense and sustained. This is not because God is reluctant to meet our needs, but because it is essential to fight our way through the fog of doubt that envelops our humanity.

The unceasing prayer that the New Testament explicitly encourages is not in order to wear down the resistance of God. He is not withholding good things from us. We pray unceasingly in order to counter our own doubt and false beliefs, our spiritual sloth and immaturity; to wear down our sense of false guilt and to resolve our real guilt; to bring our stubborn, reluctant wills into harmony with God's glorious will, so that at long last we can surmount our faulty, selfish, egocentric plans and desires, and let his wonderful love possess and transform us.

To "pray without ceasing" does not mean that we pray to the exclusion of all other activity, but rather that we keep the prayer in conscious awareness, while performing our other daily activities. It requires only a split second to tune in and affirm again and again to our souls what the mind tends to doubt. A consistent, continuous holding of our need before God is one characteristic of prayer that is answered.

Prayer must be focused. Many people, at an unconscious level, do not feel worthy to receive good things.

[64]

They may want and need love, for instance, but are incapable of accepting it when it is offered. Inwardly they do not feel worthy of love. This attitude developed in childhood in relation to one's parents and other environmental factors. We were all da-maged by our environment, to some extent, and consequently our faith is weak. It is necessary to bring our scattered emotional and spiritual forces into focus. Sometimes the only thing that will do that for us is a crisis.

Simon Peter found that a crisis brought his diffused spiritual forces into very, very fine focus one night. The disciples were out in their boat and saw a figure walking on the water. Sensing that only Jesus could perform such a feat, "Peter answered him, 'Lord, if it is you, bid me come to you on the water.' He said 'Come.' So Peter got out of the boat and walked on the water and came to Jesus; but when he saw the wind, he was afraid, and beginning to sink he cried out, 'Lord, save me.' Jesus immediately reached out his hand and caught him, saying to him, 'O man of little faith, why did you doubt?' " (Matt. 14:25-31).

Several factors in this event can claim our attention. For the moment observe two important things: Peter's impetuous and literal leap of faith and his taking a few steps on the water were the product of a moment of faith, a few seconds during which his faltering human doubts were banished by the intense emotion of the moment: seeing Jesus walking toward them on the water. He was astounded and thrilled by the implication of this power possessed by Jesus and felt challenged to emulate him. He was never a cautious man. *Impetuous* is the word most often used to describe him. I would call him emotional, impulsive, and not yet a very stable personality. But he had qualities Jesus could use—he was open and receptive, rather than a cautious doubter.

Now note one important fact often ignored: Peter actually walked on the water, however briefly. Give him credit, if only for a few moments, of transcendent faith.

If you have trouble believing that actually happened, or if you think possibly Jesus walked on the water, but Peter didn't; and if you wonder how a person in the twentieth century can take such errant nonsense literally, your argument is not with me; it is with Matthew who recorded the incident. He was there! Mark records the incident, omitting the detail of Peter's attempts to walk on the water. Mark adds, "They were utterly astounded, for they did not understand about the loaves" (Mark 6:51-52).

What Mark is suggesting, I believe, is that at this point they had forgotten how Jesus had multiplied the loaves and fishes and could not comprehend that he was master of the elements.

If that event did not transpire as recorded, then Matthew—a witness and a disciple—was either lying, exaggerating, or remembering poorly. This seems highly improbable, considering his utter devotion to Jesus and his commitment to the truth.

So, Peter's feeble, human resources were brought into intense focus by the astounding events he was experiencing. Even today people do amazing things when confronted with a crisis. The founder of one of America's largest corporations, a devout Christian layman, told me how, when he was involved in a car wreck, but uninjured, he easily lifted the car to enable a trapped passenger to escape. He was a relatively small man. He could never have performed such a feat under ordinary circumstances.

Not only is our physical strength increased in a crisis, but our spiritual and emotional resources are multiplied many times. The crisis brings it all into sharp focus.

Prayer must be in accordance with God's will. Another explicit statement in the New Testament names an important condition. It is given by John, who was there, and heard all that Jesus had to say about prayer. He could run Jesus' statements through the crucible of his mind and experience and codify them all in this profound utterance: "And this is the confidence which we have . . . that if we ask anything according to his will he hears us" (I John 5:14). The key words here are *"according to his will."*

James and John, whom Jesus humorously named Sons of Thunder, once suggested calling down fire from heaven to blot out a village which had rejected them. This petition, certainly not in harmony with the loving nature of Christ, could not be answered in the affirmative. Many of our prayers cannot be answered in the affirmative for the same reason.

A score of students are taking an examination. Let us say that all of them are praying for a much needed scholarship. Obviously God cannot grant all of those prayers. A more appropriate prayer would be for the students to pray, long weeks before the examination, to be able to do their best by way of preparation for the examination.

Two opposing athletic teams, each asking for victory, are praying amiss. They should pray only to do their best and for God's perfect will under the circumstances.

Prayer Is Not Magic

In our mechanized culture we are all familiar with and use vending machines. Stamps, cold drinks, and now even money at some banks, can be obtained from such machines. You put in a coin—or in the case of the bank machine, a special card—and out comes the merchandise or the money. Instant coffee, fast food chains, and vending machines have conditioned us to expect quick results. You push a button on your car radio and get a certain station. You put a coin in a machine and get results. You ask God for something—and nothing happens. You are disappointed and conclude that maybe God isn't real, or Jesus was misquoted, or perhaps there's nothing to prayer after all.

But prayer is not magic; it is bringing our reluctant, stubborn, sinful wills into harmony with God's will, believing that God wills our very best. The eleventh chapter of Hebrews, sometimes called the faith chapter, emphasizes the fact that prayer is not a magical way of avoiding danger and getting our desires. Let's review one small portion of that great chapter.

The author first recounts the instances when faith enabled people who trusted God to win battles, overthrow kingdoms, or be kept from harm in a den of lions. "Some, through their faith, escaped death by the sword. Some were made strong again after they had been weak or sick. Others were given great power in battles; they made whole armies turn and run away.

And some women, through faith, received their loved ones back again from death" (Heb. 11:34-35a TLB).

But, now we come to the other side of the coin:

Others trusted God and were beaten to death, preferring to die rather than turn from God and be free—trusting that they would rise to a better life afterwards.

Some were laughed at and their backs cut open with whips, and others were chained in dungeons. Some died by stoning and some by being sawed in two; others were promised freedom if they would renounce their faith, then were killed with the sword. Some went about in skins of sheep and goats, wandering over deserts and mountains, hiding in dens and caves. They were hungry and sick and ill-treated—too good for this world. And these men of faith, though they trusted God and won his approval, none of them received all that God had promised them; for God wanted them to share the even better rewards that were prepared for us. (Heb. 11;35b-40 TLB)

There it is. Some through faith triumphed and escaped danger. Others, possessing great faith, suffered unbelievable hardship and torture.

"Well," one might say, "if that's all that faith gets you, I'll just rely on my own wits and hope for the best. Prayer doesn't get you anything; at least there's no guarantee."

I am aware of no explanation anywhere in the Bible for this inescapable fact: some virtuous, devout Christians of great faith suffer; others—often less noble in nature—escape and live out their lives in ease and prosperity.

Honesty requires that we deal with this fact. Having faced both the positive and negative aspects of prayer, we return to this fact: in a crisis we all pray. When human resources fail us and disaster threatens, all humans pray. This is illustrated by the famous story of the young Russian woman who was asked on an examination what was inscribed on the tomb of Lenin. She thought she knew, but wasn't sure. She wrote, "Religion is the opiate of the people," and turned in her paper. Then she rushed to the tomb to see if she had answered correctly. She read the inscription, and found she was right. She heaved a sigh of relief and said, "Thank God!"

We do not know for sure why some prayers are answered in the affirmative, and others which also seem to be in accord with God's will are not; why there appears to be an almost capriciousness in this matter. But we do know that God is not capricious and that he does not play favorites. We must face the fact: there are some missing factors, some aspects of prayer with which we are unfamiliar.

Angry at God?

One last point. Prayer does not consist of saying the "right things" to God.

A young woman wrote me as follows:

In my Christian background we were taught never to question the will of God. I remember vividly a story told about a farmer illustrating this point. A freak cloudburst destroyed his crop a few days before he was ready to harvest it. He ran out of his home shaking his fist in the air in anger toward God. Instantly he was struck dead by lightning. The application of the story was very simple—don't question God and don't ever be angry at him.

So, for many years I covered up my legitimate questions,

and my anger, with a lot of theological rationalizations and sanctimonious prayers.

Fortunately, one day I discovered a great truth. The real feelings I had toward God surged to the surface and came out in an angry verbal torrent—and then I held my breath at the realization of what I had done. I waited for the lightning to strike me. To my considerable surprise it didn't.

I have discovered some wonderful truths—that God appreciates my honesty even if it is expressed in anger, more than beautiful, sanctimonious words which I do not feel, and which are therefore an outright lie. I have also discovered that when I allow myself to deal honestly with my true feelings, even the negative ones, eventually I get to the place where I really want to praise and thank God. I have come to understand David so much better; he who could begin a psalm with an angry outpouring of anger and vengeance, and a few verses later be singing God's praises. To discover that God's love for me is totally unaffected by my negative emotions gives me genuine cause for praise.

Also, it has helped me discover that many of the emotions I had attributed to God were really feelings that my parents expressed toward me; and most of my anger at God was really leftover anger from childhood toward my parents and other authority figures.

We are thrust back on the oft-repeated statement in the Old Testament. It is phrased in various ways, but the import is this: "You will seek me and find me; when you seek me with your whole heart" (Jer. 29:13). This brings us back again, then, to the need to give up all our halfhearted, diffused, wishful-thinking praying, and to concentrate our minds and wills on wanting God's beautiful, glorious, wonderful will. Then, when we want nothing in all the world as much as his will, we will accept healing, ease, comfort, prosperity, friends, and all the good things of life with gratitude and humility. And we will accept despair, loneliness, poverty, and defeat with equanimity, knowing that this lifetime is but the blink of an eye in the infinite plan of God, who has planned for us a paradise where every wrong is righted, the scales are balanced, and we shall "reign for ever and ever" (Rev. 22:5).

5

Prayer and Positive Thinking

"All things are possible to him who believes."
—*Mark 9:23*

In the last chapter we looked at some of the conditions Jesus gave us that must be met before we can claim Jesus' promises about getting what we ask for. We also looked at some of the characteristics of prayer.

In this chapter I'd like to go back and look in more detail at the relationship between faith and answered prayer.

Does Prayer Work?

Dr. Platon Collip, chief of pediatrics at the Nassau County Medical Center in New York, set up an experiment, using two groups of young people suffering from acute leukemia, a cancer-like disease of the blood.

One group, made up of ten patients, was the control group. The names of the other group were given to ten families in a prayer circle composed of the doctor's friends. Each family received the name of one leukemia patient for whom they were to pray daily over a fifteen-month period. The control group received no such prayers.

To rule out the possibility of suggestion, Dr. Collip did not tell any of the leukemia patients that they were being prayed for. (It is a known medical fact . . . that as many as 40 percent of patients will improve after receiving a placebo, a dummy pill, which they believe to be a potent medicine.)

Of the ten patients who received daily prayer, seven were still alive after fifteen months. Of those who were not prayed for, only two were alive after the same period.

Dr. Collip added, "It is my opinion that the results of this experiment support the view that prayer is efficacious." (*The Spiritual Frontier*, William V. Rauscher, Doubleday & Co., 1975)

Healing involves more than prayer, however. When something significant is done to assist a sick person to have a more positive attitude, the results are often astonishing. An illustration of this is the case of a man dying of generalized lymphoma. He demanded and received Krebiozon, a controversial drug which had been widely promoted as a cancer cure. Two days after the first injection the large tumors on his body had shrunk considerably, and after ten days of treatment he was discharged from the hospital.

A few months later he read reports that said the drug was worthless, and he suffered a relapse. His doctor tried to reassure him, telling him that the reports were unreliable and offering to give him a new "super refined" form of Krebiozon. Actually the physician gave him simple injections of distilled water. The patient now staged a dramatic recovery and continued to be in good health for two months. Then he read a report by the American Medical Association saying that the drug was useless as a cancer cure. His faith in the drug was shattered, and he died two days later.

Dr. Jerome D. Frank, professor emeritus of psychiatry at the Johns Hopkins School of Medicine, writes

As an example of the effect of a doctor's words in promoting expectant faith we have the case of one physician's handling of three hospitalized female patients, all in their 60s, who had not been helped by medical treatment. One woman was suffering from chronic gallbladder inflammation; the second had failed to recuperate after an operation for pancreatitis and was wasting away; and the third had inoperable cancer of the uterus, along with edema of the legs, and anemia. As an experiment, the doctor called in a faith healer—who practiced his wonders on an absentee basis—without informing the patients. After twelve healing sessions, there was no change in the patients' condition. Then the doctor told the patients that the faith healer, who was described in glowing terms, would be working for them each morning for three days, when in fact he would *not* be. The three women experienced an immediate lessening of symptoms, and all were able to leave the hospital within a week's time. The patient with pancreatitis actually got out of bed after the first healing session, rapidly gained thirty pounds, and remained well. Most amazingly, the cancer patient was able to return home after five days; her edema had disappeared and her red-blood-cell level had risen. She was able to function normally until her death several months later. Here we have a graphic illustration of how faith in a cure can be healing even when that faith is not objectively justifiable. (*Human Nature*, August 1978)

Dr. Frank points out that a placebo (an inert substance) can at times be even more effective than medication. He describes a double-bind experiment (in which neither the doctor nor the patient knew who received the drug and who received the placebo) involving the use of tranquilizers in the treatment of chronic psychiatric patients.

The experiment was run twice, using different sets of patients and different doses of both the active drug and the placebo. In the first run the patients taking the real medication (Stellazine) had an improvement rate of thirty-two percent . . . ; for those receiving the placebo the improvement rate was thirty-five percent. During the second run the dosages of placebo and drug were doubled; patients given Stallazine had an improvement rate of sixty-seven percent, while the group given a placebo had a seventy-two percent rate of improvement.

The studies indicate that in many cases, particularly in those involving a person's state of mind, the effect of medication is influenced by the hope of a cure, coupled with a belief in the physician, who in some unknown way conveys his sense of the strength and effectiveness of the drug. (*Human Nature*, August 1978)

In these experiments there were no prayers, only faith and expectation.

"Your Faith Has Made You Well"

The Gospel of Mark tells us about the woman who had been hemorrhaging for twelve years.

She had suffered much from many doctors through the years and had become poor from paying them, and was no better but, in fact, was worse. She had heard all about the wonderful miracles Jesus did, and that is why she came up behind him through the crowd and touched his clothes.

For she thought to herself, "If I can just touch his clothing, I will be healed." And sure enough, as soon as she had touched him, the bleeding stopped and she knew she was well!

Jesus realized at once that healing power had gone out from him, so he turned around in the crowd and asked, "Who touched my clothes?"

His disciples said to him, "All this crowd pressing around you, and you ask who touched you?"

But he kept on looking around to see who it was who had done it. Then the frightened woman, trembling at the realization of what had happened to her, came and fell at his feet and told him what she had done. And he said to her, "Daughter, *your faith* has made you well; go in peace, healed of your disease." (Mark 5:26-34 TLB, italics added)

There are two very significant facts here. First, Jesus took no direct action. He did not heal her with a word, a gesture, or a touch. He was totally unaware of her presence until he perceived that healing power had gone out of him. It was *her* touch, not his.

Second, when he discovered the woman who had touched him, he said, "Your faith has made you well." It was not so much Jesus, but *her own faith in Jesus* that healed her.

These and similar instances would seem to suggest that an unquestioning positive belief is the active ingredient in healing. All the necessary principles for healing are in operation, awaiting man's discovery and use. God has already set in motion the means by which all our needs can be met. Millions of years before men ever dreamed of water power, the rivers were there waiting for them to discover the marvel of hydroelectric power. Before anyone understood the laws of aerodynamics, and began to fly, the physical laws governing flight were in operation. When you cut yourself, you need not pray that the blood will coagulate and the healing process will begin. God has taken the initiative and waits for our cooperation.

This raises an important question, Is the faith of which Jesus speaks a belief that healing is going to occur, is it faith in God, or a combination of both? Is it God who brings the event to pass, or is it the faith of the pray-er? Has God built into the universe a "faith principle," which will work for anyone who has the capacity for faith? Theologians differ on the subject. I suspect that your opinion is probably as good as theirs, once you have read and absorbed the teachings of Jesus on the subject.

In the case of the woman who was healed when she touched the hem of Jesus' garment, the divine healing energy was there, available, awaiting her touch. Jesus didn't have to take any action. *It was all up to her.* Her faith in Jesus' healing power was the active ingredient.

To two blind men who asked for healing, Jesus said, "According to your faith be it done to you" (Matt. 9:29). It wasn't a matter for Jesus to decide. That the sick shall be well is God's intentional will. So, Jesus assured the men that it was *all up to them.* The two blind men received their sight when they told Jesus that they believed in his power to restore their sight. God's healing power is available, but positive results depend on one's firm belief.

Barriers to Healing

During his earthly ministry, Jesus healed all who came to him. But obviously not everyone who was sick or lame or blind could get to him. One crippled man, whose friends could not get him through the crowds and into the house where Jesus was staying, took out portions of the roof and let him down with ropes, into the very room where Jesus was speaking to the crowd. But there must have been tens of thousands who could not reach him, or had not heard of him and his power to heal. So, tragically enough, they were not healed.

There are other factors. Our faith is weakened if we do not want God's will in every area of our life. We cannot have his blessings if we do not want his will. Another consideration is that unresolved guilt destroys one's capacity for faith. Guilt, which creates conflict, dissipates one's faith. Any serious ambivalence, or anxiety, seems to inhibit faith. One needs to experience faith, or belief, with all of one's nature. When there is a division or a split in one's life, faith is severely limited.

Warren, forty-five years old, is an example of both these barriers. He had been depressed all his life, as he told us when he came to the Burlingame Counseling Center. In addition, he suffered from a paralyzing indecision and severe anxiety. He was barely able to hold a job. His first wife had divorced him because of his negative personality characteristics, and a second one threatened to do so.

In desperation he talked to his minister, who recognized that Warren needed professional help. He had repeatedly tried talk therapy, but of course this is usually ineffective in dealing with deep depression and anxiety. When he came to our Counseling Center he described his fear of losing his job, his poor performance in his profession, and the very real fear that he might lose his family unless he could be helped.

We explained Primal Integration therapy to him. He wasn't a very good subject for his lifelong depression had rendered him quite unresponsive. We felt for a time that our efforts would be fruitless.

Eventually Warren began to emerge from his despair. He was driving an ancient car with 170,000 miles on it, too given to procrastination to trade it in on a new one. He had even refused to talk with his wife about it, though she was pressing for a car of more recent vintage. But before long, Warren was sufficiently relieved of his anxiety and indecision enough to go out and buy a new car.

The next step, one he had dreaded, was to consider a transfer to another firm, where he hoped for better working conditions. He had been so frozen with indecision that he had dreaded making the change.

But one day he took the plunge and got the new position. This gave him new courage. We began to notice a marvelous change in his personality. His wife came in to see me, simply to express her profound gratification at the transformation that had taken place in him. Finally, when Warren was finished with his weekly Primal Integration sessions, he was a cheerful, confident, happy individual for the first time in his forty-five years.

Warren was a Christian and a faithful church member. Primal Integration therapy, practiced in a Christian orientation, had been available for several years within a few miles of where he lived. He just had not heard of it, and so his healing was delayed. He had prayed, in his depressed way, for a solution. He had tried various forms of counseling. Why had his prayers never been answered, until age forty-five, when he was near the end of his rope? Part of the answer is that the prayers of depressed people seem to produce negative results.

We now come to two important questions. *First,* if negative belief can cause physical symptoms, to what extent can positive belief give us healing?

There are innumerable cases of individuals having succumbed to negative belief, with disastrous consequences. There is abundant evidence, too, especially at divine healing services, that positive belief can in many cases induce healing. The statement of Jesus, "According to your faith be it done to you," seems to suggest that divine energy is available to everyone. Faith appears to be the quality which releases that energy. God's love and power, plus our belief, seems to be the formula.

Second, is it God who heals, or do we heal ourselves through our faith? In the case of the self-healing wound, there seems to be no need on our part to believe in the marvelous process of coagulation that stops bleeding, followed by an intricate healing process.

In the case of instantaneous healing, it is more difficult to reduce it to a simple spiritual formula. For instance, in Kathryn Kulhman's healing services many people were healed without specifically asking for it, except that by their presence they were presumably open to it. Yet, many devout and hurting people were present in her services who were not healed.

We are dealing, not with a God who plays favorites, but with differences in temperament. Being suggestible is neither a good nor a bad trait. It is simply a temperamental difference. Some children seem to be natural believers from birth, but others are by nature less suggestible. It is an emotional/temperamental difference of genetic origin, perhaps affected in some degree by environment.

Some people find it much easier to have faith than others. Thomas, labeled "the doubter," was of a different temperament than some of the more emotionally responsive disciples. Simon Peter, who leapt out of the boat to walk on the water to Jesus had a different temperament from the others who would never have dreamed of attempting such an impetuous act.

It doesn't seem fair that some people can summon deep faith more easily than others. But then, little about life is fair. It isn't fair that one child in a family with an IQ of 130 gets straight As without the slightest difficulty, while a sibling with an IQ of 105 has to struggle to make passing grades; and a third child becomes a musical genius, while a fourth can't carry a tune.

Jesus dealt with this inequity. He said, "Much is required from those to whom much is given, for their responsibility is greater" (Luke 12:48*b* TLB). This explains a great deal, but it is small comfort to the person who suffers from a serious illness, or is confronted by some problem for which there seems no answer. The knowledge that others have been given greater capacity for faith, and he less, simply compounds his feelings of defeat and hopelessness.

When the Larger Prayer Is Answered

We need to make one final comment about faith and answered prayer. Sometimes God says no to our specific request so he can answer the real prayer of our hearts.

Monica, mother of Augustine, was deeply distressed. Her willful son announced his intention of leaving their home on the north coast of Africa and going to live in Rome.

The Eternal City was known throughout the civilized world as the center of every conceivable form of licentiousness. Monica prayed earnestly that her son would change his mind. But headstrong Augustine defied his mother's wishes and journeyed to Rome. After a brief fling, he fell under the influence of one of the most remarkable bishops of the early church. He became a Christian, and eventually the most outstanding Christian leader of the day. His writings are still read today. Monica's specific prayer had gone unanswered, but the broader prayer for her son's ultimate welfare was granted.

Jesus prayed in the Garden of Gethsemane, "My Father, if it be possible, let this cup pass from me; nevertheless, not as I will, but as thou wilt" (Matt. 26:39). His humanity understandably recoiled from the horror of the cross; another aspect of his nature sought the ultimate—God's will.

We pray, in desperation or pain, for a specific answer to our problem. That specific prayer may not be granted, and only in long-term retrospect can we sometimes see that the larger prayer for our total good was granted.

Starting in high school, I worked my way through a seemingly interminable number of years, ending with graduate school. At one point I spent eight hours a day for a month, looking for a part-time job. Jobs were very scarce then. I sometimes prayed for a lessening of the burden. That petition was not granted; but as I look back from the vantage point of the years, I can see that I needed desperately the experience gained by working my way through school. I learned innumerable lessons not taught in the classroom. Without that experience life later would have been immeasurably more difficult.

I am confident that only with the clarity of vision and wisdom granted us in heaven will we ever understand the reason for some of our unanswered prayers. At that point, no doubt, we will be able to exclaim, "Oh, now it's so clear! In his infinite love God saw what was best."

Often referred to as the most patient man in the Bible, Job was not always uncomplaining and trusting. He chided God, "Why dost thou hide thy face? (Job 13:24*a*). There was no possible way he could make any sense out of the incredible multiple tragedies that had befallen him.

A bit later he cries triumphantly, though still in utmost misery of mind, body, and circumstances: "I know that my Redeemer lives" (Job 19:25). Finally, toward the end of the story, we are told, "When Job prayed for his friends, the Lord restored his wealth and happiness! In fact, the Lord gave him twice as much as before!" (Job 42:10 TLB).

Not every story in the Bible has such a happy ending. Many faithful Christians have endured imprisonment, torture, and martyrdom. Tradition has it that the apostle Paul was beheaded, just outside Rome on the Appian Way, after a long imprisonment. Some of the Twelve were killed, and uncounted thousands of early Christians suffered persecution and martyrdom.

Here, then, is another of the mysteries—the question as to why the righteous suffer, their prayers unanswered, while evil flourishes. And this is where faith comes in: not in simply believing a set of doctrines *about* God, but trusting him and sensing that in the end the scales will be balanced, for God is just. One day the mystery will become clear. Justice and mercy and love and truth will triumph. Faith is believing *that!*

6

What Can One Believe About God, Christ, and the Holy Spirit?

When you get out there a quarter of a million miles away from home, you look at earth with a little different perspective. The earth looks so perfect. There are no strings to hold it up, no fulcrum upon which it rests. You think of the infinity of time . . . I didn't see God. But I am convinced of God by the order out in space. I know it didn't happen by accident.

—*Eugene A. Cernan, Apollo 17 astronaut*

What can one believe? Is there any core of belief to which one can cling, some set of basic fundamentals upon which one can build his own set of values and regulate his conduct?

The longer I live the more firmly I believe in certain things. Experience has validated them for me, and I see them being confirmed in the lives of others. Here are some of the basic beliefs which I now hold.

God, the Creator of All

God is. A creation implies a creator. A design requires a designer. It seems to me self-evident that God exists. In fact, one of the names God reveals in the

Old Testament is I AM. The God whom most atheists or agnostics reject is the God of their childhood—a frowning, punitive deity, or one who can be cajoled into granting one's special requests—not the God of creation, the God of the Bible.

One can never know all about God, any more than one can explore and know all the shores of all the oceans. The finite cannot know the infinite, yet may understand some things about it.

God can be known, but he cannot be fully understood. We can know some things about him, which Jesus revealed to us and which we find in the Bible, but they are surely an infinitesimal fraction of the infinite mind of God.

For instance, a child of three knows that his father loves her, sets limits, punishes, and rewards her. But the three-year-old is utterly incapable of understanding all the ramifications of her father's world. How can a child understand a manufacturing plant, with a thousand employees; or an accounting firm with reams of paper and unintelligible figures; or a sales organization with training courses, quotas, and a product to be sold; or an office filled with computers, balance sheets, and profit and loss statements; or the work of a mechanic who services an automobile with hundreds of intricate parts?

Just as children are incapable of comprehending all the manifold intricacies of their father's world, so we humans are unable to understand the vast reaches of God's mind and universe.

God reveals himself in his creation. Meister Eckhart, fifteenth-century mystic, declares that God makes a thing by becoming that thing. God does not dwell in splendid isolation in some far-off corner of his universe, but indwells every blade of grass, every atom, every amoeba, and each drop of water. He expresses himself in the sunset, as in every aspect of nature. (This is not pantheism, the idea that God is the sum total of all creation, but pan*en*theism, the concept that God indwells all creation, but is an entity apart from creation.) He reveals himself in humankind, who is capable of communicating with his creator. Supremely, God is revealed in Jesus.

I knew a young woman who had suffered deeply as the result of her rebellion against the laws of God and man. She had totally rejected the love of her family. Then, finally, in despair and disillusionment she returned home. Like the prodigal son, she had come to herself.

Back in college again, she wrote me from time to time. In one letter which I have treasured for its sheer beauty she wrote:

Dear Dr. Osborne:
Sometimes a thing happens to me and I just must tell someone. I will tell you because you're the only one I really feel will understand—and because you are my friend.

Every once in a while a feeling comes to me—the feeling of intense love or passion for parts of life. When I walk to class through the park the pine trees are so wonderfully tall, and sway as if they embrace one another. The crocuses and daffodils are so purely yellow and live so simply. The grass is so green and lush, and all the joys of loving and being in love just melt together, and all I do is sit and cry—cry because the feeling is so warm and alive and total that I can't wholly grasp it. The rhythms, motions, colors of life so astound me that I can only guess at the genius of its Creator. This must be a gift—a token of his way of expressing the goodness that he is for us—that he would heal the scars that life gives us, and that he cares so dearly for us.

My love, S———

God is spirit. The concept that God indwells all that he has created, yet is an entity apart from his creation, does not make him an impersonal force. Yet to say that he is a "person," or "personal," limits him. Jesus at no time described God as a person. Rather, he said, "God is spirit." I do not know what spirit is. I can perceive only how spirit is manifested. I see God, Spirit, manifesting himself in nature, and in us. He becomes personal in persons. One aspect of his nature is that he feels, wills, loves as humans do, only to a limitless degree.

He is a loving God. Just as small children may not understand everything about their father but know they are loved, so we know that the heavenly Father loves us. We see it manifested in the matchless life of Jesus, who said, "He who has seen me has seen the Father" (John 14:9*b*).

No other world religion with which I am familiar proclaims such a God of love. One may know intellectually many things *about* God, yet not know him. A person may know intellectually that God is omnipotent, omnipresent, and omniscient, but he or she can know God only through love.

The young woman who wrote so beautifully of her sensing God in nature wrote me on another occasion. I was thrilled by a closing phrase in her letter: "I am believing good things for you through our loving Father. Toward a more joyous, useful life through the unbelievably wonderful power of our Father through love. Your friend, S———."

She did not love him because she knew *about* him. She knew him because she loved him.

She was perceiving God through love, sensing him, feeling him, letting him speak to her and through her. The most learned theologian could not convey the love of God to me as deeply as my young friend did through her letter.

Jesus Christ, Vice-Regent of God

Christ is the God of our planet, and for all we know, of other planets as well. Jesus declared, "All authority in heaven and on earth has been given to me" (Matt. 28:18). I take that to mean that Jesus, to put it simply, became the vice-regent of God the Father. Jesus does not make any claim to *being* God, but simply that they are one. "My Father and I are one" (John 10:30 NEB) implies that Jesus was at one with the Father, in perfect harmony with him. God is like Jesus.

Yes, the only God I expect to see in heaven is Christ, to whom all power and authority was given on this earth, and in the heaven which pertains to this earth. It is quite possible, of course, that Christ may be Lord of the known universe, and that there may be other universes scattered throughout infinite space. The apostle Paul seems to imply this in his letters.

Listen to Paul's glorious description of Jesus. Read it slowly, then read it again to get the full effect. Let it sink in.

[God] has delivered us from the dominion of darkness and transferred us to the kingdom of his beloved Son, in whom we have redemption, the forgiveness of sin.

He is the image of the invisible God, the first-born of all creation; for in him all things were created, in heaven and on earth, visible and invisible, whether thrones or dominions or principalities or authorities—all things were created through him and for him. He is before all things, and in him all things hold together. He is the head of the body, the church; he is the beginning, the first-born from the dead, that in everything he might be pre-eminent. For in him all the fulness of God was pleased to dwell, and through him to reconcile to himself all things, whether on earth or in heaven, making peace by the blood of his cross. (Col. 1:13-20)

The Living Bible translates the first part of the above paragraph, "Christ is the exact likeness of the unseen God. He existed before God made anything at all, and, in fact, Christ himself is the Creator who made everything in heaven and earth, the things we can see and the things we can't."

Jesus the man—a secular picture. Occasionally a secular writer hits the nail on the head better, and expresses it more succinctly, than some of the rest of us. For instance, this condensed version of the life of Christ was written by Charles McCabe in the *San Francisco Chronicle* (December 22, 1980):

Because of those silly Roman laws, the couple, who were traveling to the husband's hometown, had to check in at an inn to comply with a census the Romans were taking.

They found there was no room for them, and their child was born in the nearest and warmest place they could find, which was a stable in the town of Bethlehem, Judea.

The boy, who was descended from David through his father's line, probably followed his father's trade and worked as a carpenter and joiner.

His spiritual life really began when he was 30 or so, and he was baptized by his cousin, a pretty revolutionary fellow called John the Baptist. John believed in repentance and forgiveness, and denounced Herod Antipas for divorcing his wife and taking a new one. The daughter of Herod's new wife, Salome, asked for John's head, and got it.

The young man, named Jesus, carried on the mission of John, and brought his teachings to their logical conclusion.

This fellow Jesus said things like this:

"Love your enemies." "Ye cannot serve God and Mammon." "Therefore, all things whatsoever ye would that men should do to you, do ye even so to them; for this is the law and the prophets."

He was doing that most revolutionary of things, using love as a political weapon.

With Herod watching, he drove the moneylenders from the temple, and performed miracles on the Sabbath, and hung around with a questionable crowd, which included publicans and sinners. His worst sin in the eyes of the procurator of Judea was the Sermon on the Mount. After that, a contract was out for Jesus.

After living in Tyre and Sidon, Jesus returned in triumph to Jerusalem during the week of the Passover. He had a meal with his twelve disciples, and was betrayed by one of them with a kiss.

The ruling clique, who knew they had to get rid of this strange and loving man, fixed it up so that he was condemned to death after a hurried trial. He was crucified and his followers deserted him.

The cross upon which he died became the symbol of his teachings and remains so today.

No western man alive today, whatever his religious persuasion, or lack of it, can say that his life has not been affected, and deeply, by Jesus Christ.

Christianity, as of today, is still but a promise, but how bleak our life would be without that promise!

We are too imperfect to love our neighbor just because we are told to do so, and just because we know we should. Yet we do know that we should, and in that sense Christianity has been a success, if not a triumph.

We are not ready, yet, for the teachings of Christ. It is my hope, and I trust it is not a deluded one, that we each day become more ready.

Perhaps the only way we will become Christians is by being frightened into it by that big dread black bullet called the atom bomb.

However we make it, there is something deep in our natures that deserves Christ and His teachings. If we have to be frightened into his arms, this, too, is an irony that Jesus of Nazareth would have appreciated.

That pretty well sums it up, doesn't it?

Jesus, the challenger. In his novel, *Act of God*, Charles Templeton tells about Michael, who picked up Goodspeed's translation of the New Testament in modern English, took it with him to bed and read the four Gospels straight through. It seemed almost a revelation, and so excited him that he lay still in bed, wide-eyed until dawn.

The man in the text was unlike the Christ he'd heard declaimed about for as long as he could remember. This wasn't the effeminate, vacant-faced figure of stained glass windows nor the impeccably robed, perfectly coiffed refugee from a Cecil B. De Mille movie he'd seen reproduced in church school literature. And how different the familiar sayings seemed when they emerged from *his* lips. Gentle Jesus, meek and mild—nonsense! This was a revolutionary of astounding commitment: strong, opinionated, contentious, impatient and often quick-tempered. He showed no slightest interest in turning away with a soft answer; indeed, he frequently provoked his enemies. He challenged the religious power structure of his time and confounded the authorities in every confrontation. Nor was he aloof: he was gregarious, much given to dining out—whether in the homes of the riffraff or the respectable didn't seem to matter; but so indifferent to protocol that he was sometimes rebuked for not troubling to wash before meals. Yet, there remained the paradox: for all his sociability he was a loner.

The real Jesus. The young man's picture of Jesus may not be yours, but it does have the merit of stripping from the real Jesus much of the fake trappings with which artists and writers have endowed him through the centuries. I particularly resent, with great intensity, the calendar-type art which portrays Jesus as a supersweet, effeminate creature walking through the daisies with a pretty little lamb in his arms. Such a person could never have stood up to the Pharisees and called them, repeatedly, hypocrites, white sepulchures, generation of vipers. A meek and mild Jesus would never have told the Jews the parable of the good Samaritan, since Jews regarded Samaritans worse than outcasts. To cast a despised Samaritan in the role of hero was to think the unthinkable. That took courage!

Jesus calls for commitment. Jesus called disciples to follow him and obey his teaching. And he commissioned them to make other disciples, so that his call for followers reaches to us today. "Believe in God; believe also in me," is his challenge.

If you are delaying a commitment to Christ until you understand how he fed the five thousand, or stilled the waves, or healed the sick and raised the dead, you will never arrive at a decision. If I had delayed my first plane flight until I understood the workings of a 747, I would never have flown. I never board one of those monsters but that I say to myself, "This thing will never get off the ground." That is my emotional reaction. I simply do not understand how it can lift that vast plane load of people and fling them to another continent. But it does, and I don't have to understand how it is accomplished. I just have to get on and trust what my intellect tells me is true. It is an act of faith. I have no real assurance that it will get me to my destination, other than the statistical evidence.

The only proof we have that Jesus rose from the dead is the testimony of those who saw him. The assurance we have concerning eternal life is the statement of Jesus, "Because I live, you will live also" (John 14:19*b*).

The Trinity

No subject has created so much controversy and generated as much confusion among Christians as the Trinity. Theologians have debated the subject for generations. Some who disagreed with the accepted view in the past were burned at the stake for their alleged heresy.

My own views on the subject could well have sent me to the torture rack, or to the stake, in medieval Europe. Admittedly my view may be out of the mainstream of standard interpretations, but I am confident that any honest theological error concerning the Trinity is not going to affect my salvation or that of anyone else.

A "Committee God"? A pagan, with many gods, if introduced suddenly to Christianity might see little difference between his many deities and our Trinity of divine beings—Father, Son, and Holy Spirit—and in the case of Roman Catholics, a host of saints to whom one may pray. This is a far cry from the Old Testament assertion, "Hear, O Israel: The Lord our God is one Lord" (Deut. 6:4*a*).

See if you can understand this bit of ancient erudition which seeks to explain how the early Christian scholars differed on the subject of the Trinity:

Some said that there was but one substance in the God-head, others, three. Some allowed the terms . . . according as they were guided by the prevailing heresy of the day and their own judgment concerning it. . . . Some declare that God is numerically three; others numerically one; while to others it might appear more philosophical to exclude ideas of numbers altogether in the discussion of that mysterious Nature which is beyond comparison, whether viewed as One, or Three, and neither falls under nor forms any conceivable species. (*The Aryans of the Fourth Century*, ed. 1854)

Does that enlighten you?

The Council of Nicea tried in A.D. 325 to settle the matter with a specific declaration three hundred years after the crucifixion; but no one has cleared it up satisfactorily, or made the matter of the Trinity understandable to the average person. Many Christians have just gone on believing it without pretending to understand what it is all about.

God is one. Granted that mine is rather a simplistic answer, it solves the problem for me, at least for the moment: God is one, not three. The Bible nowhere uses the word Trinity. He is the one universal, uncreated Source, Sustainer, and Creator, without beginning or end. He has always been.

The Spirit of God, which is holy. Jesus is the God of our world, the vice-regent of our planet (and conceivably of the universe). Let us say that the Holy Spirit, instead of being the "third person of the Trinity," which is not stated in the Bible, is the "Spirit of God, which is holy," one of the means by which God manifests himself through his universe. The Holy Spirit is the power of God: "I am full of power by the spirit of the Lord, and of judgment and of might," declares the prophet Micah (3:8 KJV).

Much misunderstanding arises over the fact that the Holy Spirit is often referred to as "he," which would imply a specific personality. Jesus referred to the Holy Spirit as "the Comforter." "Comforter," *parakletos*, is masculine in Greek, just as are many inanimate objects, and Greek rules of grammar require the use of a masculine pronoun to refer to a masculine noun. This explains why "he" is used in some instances where reference is to "the Comforter."

At his baptism, all three aspects of the nature of God were manifested: "And when Jesus was baptized, he went up immediately from the water, and behold, the heavens were opened and he saw the Spirit of God descending like a dove, and alighting on him; and lo, a voice from heaven, saying, 'This is my beloved Son, with whom I am well pleased' " (Matt. 3:16-17).

Here is the Son being baptized before entering his ministry, the Spirit of God descending, manifested in some manner that evoked the image of a dove, and the voice of God identifying Jesus as the Son of God and expressing his pleasure in him.

Scholars have argued and debated for nearly two thousand years about this subject, and it would be monumentally presumptuous of me to attempt to clarify in a few paragraphs a subject that will perhaps remain a mystery to our finite minds.

Three roles or manifestations. Perhaps a few simple analogies will assist in grasping the idea. I am a son, a husband, and a father. I act in all three roles, but I am one person. A different aspect of my personality functions in each of the roles, but I remain distinctly one individual.

Or one might think of H_2O, which can be manifested as water, steam, or ice. Each appears and feels radically different, and has different functions, though they consist of one basic essence.

Now, let it be said that either of these two analogies would at one time or another in Christian history have been considered heretical; but rest assured that your own private interpretation of the mystery of the Trinity, whether it be ultimately true or false, theologically correct or pathetically childish, will in no way affect your eternal destiny.

Truth Hidden from the Wise

Matthew records a most instructive and interesting prayer of Jesus: "O Father, Lord of heaven and earth, thank you for hiding the truth from those who think themselves so wise, and for revealing it to little children. Yes, Father, for it pleased you to do it this way!" (Matt. 11:25-26 TLB).

While the learned theologians have sought fruitlessly for nearly two thousand years to explain the Trinity satisfactorily, the average Christian has just gone on saying, "I don't understand the Trinity," not bothering much about the esoteric explanation of the scholars. Much as a homeowner uses electrical power without having the slightest idea where the powerhouse is, or how it operates, or what electricity is (which no one really understands anyhow), a Christian can have a beautiful and gratifying relationship with the Father, can love and obey Jesus, and can be guided by the Spirit of God, which is Holy.

Jesus was not depreciating education or intelligence when he thanked God that "children"—the uneducated and naïve—were granted power to understand what the intellectuals could not grasp. He was simply enunciating an oft-forgotten principle—the relatively unsophisticated mind is often more capable of a deep and satisfying faith than the overeducated intellect.

Jesus thanked God for this, as, in mixed sorrow and anger, he turned from the great cities and began to minister more exclusively to the common people in the rural and small town areas, who "heard him gladly" (Mark 12:37 KJV).

It seems much easier for us to relate to Jesus, a human entity, than to the more nebulous Holy Spirit. And perhaps this is as it should be.

Jesus can be visualized. He walked the earth, touched lives, spoke matchless truths, and manifested a divine love which no other person has ever done. We may experience the power of the Holy Spirit, but we can visualize Jesus.

He transcends all other religious figures. In one sense, he didn't have much to do with religion. He spoke of life, love, relationships, eternal life, and God's loving concern for us.

His assurance of eternal life is validated by his resurrection and his appearance to over five hundred persons afterward.

He lures us toward the ultimate goal of perfection, but offers acceptance and forgiveness when we fail.

His example confirms his teachings in marvelous ways.

On the cross he revealed the unconditional love of which he had spoken, when he forgave those who hung him on a cross to die a shameful and agonizing death. God in Christ manifested the kind of love that is at the heart of the universe.

In his daily life he revealed moral grandeur and spiritual perfection unrivaled by any other religious leader.

He exposed the hypocrisy of the Pharisees with words that blistered and burned, and exploded with rage as he cast the moneychangers out of the temple, yet he knelt to gaze with exquisite tenderness into the eyes of a terrified woman flung at his feet.

He was betrayed by one disciple, denied by another, doubted by a third, and abandoned by them all at the end; yet after the resurrection, he dealt with them in exquisite gentleness.

There is something unique about him; something that challenges us, rebukes us, and loves us all at the same time. Our minds may boggle at the concept of the Trinity, but Jesus we can understand, love, and do our feeble, faltering best to follow. For no one has ever exhibited such love as he. And his love, far more than complex theological truths, is what matters. For God in Christ is love. His love reaches out to us, gently, powerfully, redemptively. Who, but one determined on a course of self-destruction, could resist that love?

7

What About Miracles?

It was said of one zealous apostle of free thought that he would believe anything so long as it was not in the Bible.

—Gordon Allport

From the cowardice that shrinks from new truth,
From the laziness that is content with half-truth,
From the arrogance that thinks it knows all truth,
Oh, God of Truth, deliver us!

—Ancient Hebrew Prayer

Did Jesus *actually walk on the water, or was that* a myth which grew up about him, created by *overzealous disciples?*

Did he raise Lazarus *from the dead,* or was that simply a story that his ardent disciples spread *in an attempt to prove his divinity?*

Did he literally *heal people with a touch,* or did he relieve them of their *neuroses?*

Did *he feed the five thousand with a few loaves* (actually rolls) and fishes, or is that an *allegory, describing the manner* in which he broke the bread of truth *to his followers?*

[101]

Was *Jesus born of a virgin, or* is the story an effort to cloak his birth with an aura of *mystery and divinity?*

Let us deal with these and other questions which are legitimately raised concerning the recorded miracles.

The Power of a Higher Law

A miracle is usually defined as an event contrary to the laws of nature, worked by a superhuman agency as a manifestation of its power. I have not the slightest difficulty believing that Jesus performed the acts—called miracles—ascribed to him. However, I do not call them miracles, for by definition such an act is "contrary to natural law." I prefer to believe that Jesus healed and performed the other so-called miracles, not by violating natural law, but by *invoking a higher law* than the ones with which we are familiar.

For instance, steel does not float, but by invoking a higher law it floats when formed into a ship. An airplane does not violate the law of gravity, but flies because it is in harmony with the higher law of aerodynamics. The higher law does not violate, but supersedes the lesser or prior law.

Jesus seems to have healed, with a word or touch, or at a distance, by pouring the torrent of his love into the life of the sick person. He was able to do this, not because he had sole access to some miracle-working power, but because he used powers available to us. He said to his disciples, "Truly, truly, I say to you, he who believes in me will also do the work that I do; and greater works than these will he do, because I go to my Father" (John 14:12). He lived without the inner conflicts that rob us of a large portion of our spiritual and psychic energy. Saying this in no way robs Christ of his divinity.

Guilt, in essence, is trying to pursue incompatible moral goals, and this produces conflict. Jesus had no such inner conflicts; he fully accepted both his divinity and his humanity. In total obedience to the Father he had access to powers which are equally available to those who totally accept their humanity and their divinity, and are fully obedient to the Father. No one else has ever achieved this.

J. B. Phillips translates Ephesians 1:19-20: "How tremendous is *the power available to us* who believe in God. That power is the same divine energy which was demonstrated in Christ when he raised him from the dead and gave him the place of supreme honor in Heaven" (emphasis added). This stresses the fact that the power which raised Jesus on resurrection day *is available to us!*

Jesus' state of spiritual development enabled him to heal the sick, multiply the loaves and the fishes, yes, and to still the waves. Surely these are no greater feats just because they seem more difficult to our guilt-ridden minds. The wonder these events produced was no greater than the amazement which would be expressed by my grandfather if he could return and watch on a TV broadcast events that occur on the far side of the earth, or with four hundred fifty other passengers ride in a 747 jet six miles above the earth, at five hundred fifty miles an hour. To him that would be a mind-boggling event, a supermiraculous event scarcely to be believed.

Our small granddaughter was with me in the car when I pressed a button that made the large garage door begin to rise. She clapped her hands in glee and said ecstatically, "Oh, look, a magic door!" She then turned immediately to talk about something else. She had no difficulty accepting the fact that a door opened "magically," though she did not have the slightest idea of how it happened. So she labeled it magic. The observers of Jesus' actions, not understanding how he performed them, called them "wonders," or "miracles."

The Miracles Cannot Be Discarded

We cannot exclude the miracles from the biblical account any more than we can with impunity discard the account of the Sermon on the Mount or the crucifixion. The New Testament records seventeen instances of healing. Many more were lumped together, for we read that on numerous occasions crowds gathered and Jesus "healed all of the sick."

Three people were raised from the dead, and six people experienced exorcisms. Half a dozen times Jesus demonstrated his power over nature.

The rational mind tends to exclude the idea that events can transpire outside of one's own experience. Thomas had such a mind-set. After the resurrection when Jesus first appeared to his disciples, Thomas was absent. When the eleven told him that they had seen the Lord, Thomas responded, "Unless I see in his hands the print of the nails, and place my finger in the mark of the nails, and place my hand in his side, I will not believe" (John 20:25). John tells us that eight days later all the disciples were together again when Jesus appeared to them. Jesus said to Thomas, "Put your finger here, and see my hands; and put out your hand, and place it in my side; do not be faithless, but believing." Thomas did so, then exclaimed, "My Lord, and my God!" (John 20:27). His type of mind required visual and tactile proof.

Dr. Robert B. Greenblatt, who has achieved international recognition for his remarkable accomplishments in medicine, has written a highly interesting book title, *Search the Scriptures* (J. B. Lippincott & Co., 1977), in which he deals with science and the Bible. Though a Jew, he accepts without question the fact that Jesus performed the miracles of healing ascribed to him, including the exorcism of evil spirits. He writes:

Jesus knew that sickness is often the manifestation of a disturbed soul. To the man sick with palsy he said, not "arise and walk," but preferring to put his mind at ease, "Thy sins be forgiven thee."

Jesus' ministry was to the total human need. He knew what we have come to realize only recently: that much of our illness comes from broken interpersonal relations, from guilt and from the void where no love is. His earliest doctrine linked preaching with healing: "Heal the sick, cleanse the lepers, raise the dead, cast out devils."

To the skeptic, any pronouncement of science becomes an established fact, even if it has not yet been documented, whereas the miracles that Jesus performed automatically become suspect because they are recorded in the Bible.

A scientist has pointed out that astronauts traveling at 99 percent of the speed of light can go to the star Procyon (10.4 light years away) and back in twenty-one years. To the astronauts it would seem that only three years had passed, but on earth, everyone would be twenty-one years older. I read that, accept it on faith in the scientist who has it all figured out, but I do not understand the principle, which is that time slows down for an object moving near the speed of light. What perversity of the human minds is it that makes it so easy to give ready assent to any scientific declaration and so reluctant to accept biblical truth?

Jesus was aware both of people's gullibility and their skepticism. He was reluctant at the outset to have word of his healings spread abroad and warned one leper to tell no one. But he said to a disciple, "Believe me that I am in the Father and the Father in me; or else believe me for the sake of the works themselves" (John 14:11). If they could not believe him because of his teachings, he urged them to believe, if for no other reason, because of the people they saw being healed with a touch or a word.

The Virgin Birth

It is difficult for many people to accept the virgin birth. Skeptics point out that the mother of Hercules was supposedly a virgin; and Attis was allegedly born of a virgin, as were Bacchus, Aesculapius, Buddha, Zarathustra, and numerous others. The argument is that having one born of a virgin would prove his divinity, making him "special." Divinity, of course, is not proven by having one parent instead of two. Evil can be transmitted through a mother as well as by a father.

Joseph was shocked at learning that Mary was pregnant, and "unwilling to put her to shame, resolved to divorce her quietly" (Matt. 1:19). We rule out the possibility that she could have become pregnant by someone other than Joseph, to whom she was betrothed. This lovely and devout young girl was not the sort. A reading of the first chapter of Luke is revealing:

In the sixth month the angel Gabriel was sent from God to a city of Galilee named Nazareth, to a virgin betrothed to a man whose name was Joseph, of the house of David; and the virgin's name was Mary. And he came to her and said, "Hail, O favored one, the Lord is with you!" But she was greatly troubled at the saying, and considered in her mind what sort of greeting this might be. And the angel said to her, "Do not be afraid, Mary, for you have found favor with God. And behold, you will conceive in your womb and bear a son, and you shall call his name Jesus.
He will be great and will be called the Son of the Most
   High;
and the Lord God will give him the throne of his father
   David,
and he will reign over the house of Jacob for ever;
and of his kingdom there will be no end."
And Mary said to the angel, "How can this be, since I have no husband?"
And the angel said to her,
"The Holy Spirit will come upon you,
and the power of the Most High will overshadow you;
therefore the child to be born will be called holy,
the Son of God. . . ."
And Mary said, "Behold, I am the handmaid of the Lord; let it be to me according to your word." And the angel departed from her. (Luke 1:26-38)

I do not for a moment believe that my salvation depends on accepting the virgin birth of Jesus. I believe it because of my belief in the integrity of the author, a physician, whose entire Gospel has the ring of truth.

Dr. Howard Kelly, one of the four founders of Johns Hopkins University and a distinguished gynecologist, wrote a book some years ago titled, *A Scientific Man and the Bible* (out of print). In one chapter he dealt with the virgin birth. I expected to find some scientific justification for the biblical account. To my considerable surprise, Dr. Kelly said, in effect, that as a gynecologist and a Christian he accepted the virgin birth of Jesus *"because it was recorded in the New Testament!"*

Vance Packard writes in *The People Sharers* (Little Brown & Co., 1977): "In higher life forms, there are recorded cases of female eggs spontaneously dividing and growing. Scientists at the U.S. Department of Agriculture spotted a strain of domestic turkey hens that has a tendency to lay hatchable eggs without benefit of semen from a tom. . . . Over several years thousands of these eggs were identified. A few dozen hatched infant turkeys. Some grew to maturity. At least one has actually sired offspring." A Harvard team "has identified 27 kinds of parthenogenetic lizards—all female species that lay eggs to produce exact genetic copies of the mother." Physiologist David Crews and a group of researchers discovered the "virgin birth" lizards in Arizona and Colorado. If some lower forms of life have parthenogenesis, there is no particular reason why it cannot occur among humans, even without divine intervention.

Virgin births of human females almost certainly have occurred spontaneously, according to one geneticist. Some years ago there was an uproar over a talk given in England by Helen Spurway, a geneticist at University College, London. On the basis of animal research, she cited figures suggesting that every year several dozen human virgin births probably occur somewhere in the world. Other estimates have since placed the estimates both higher and lower.

How does Jesus' birth differ from such presumed "virgin" births?

The Scriptures do not infer that the virgin birth of Jesus proves his divinity. Since parthenogenesis occurs in nature, among animals, and some scientists assert the probability of numerous virgin births among humans, this could conceivably resolve the doubts of some who question the inspiration of Scriptures simply because they cannot believe Luke's account of Jesus' birth.

The Star of Bethlehem

What about the star the Wise Men saw in the East which later guided them to the spot where Jesus had been born? "And lo, the star which they had seen in the East went before them, till it came to rest over the place were the child was" (Matt. 2:9).

Is this a fanciful story to make the birth of Jesus seem more magical, or was there an actual star? *The Smithsonian* (June 1979), publication of the Smithsonian Institute, states:

The star of Bethlehem has intrigued astronomers for centuries and until recently the preferred explanation was a close encounter of Jupiter and Saturn in 7 B.C. (The monks who drew up the calendar blew it; Christ was born before A.D. 1). But Jupiter and Saturn didn't get close enough to look like one star, it is argued, and now the astronomers from University College, London, and one from the University of Newcastle, have a better idea: a nova (that is, an exploding star). And in the history of the Han dynasty they found a record of a new star that shone for 70 days in the spring of the year 5 B.C.

Most Bible scholars place the birth of Jesus, on the basis of historical evidence, at either 4 or 5 B.C. This recent discovery by the English astronomers would seem to place the star at the right time historically. There had long been prophecies circulating in the Middle and Far East concerning the birth of an extraordinary king whose birth would be accompanied by a celestial phenomenon. The Wise Men, undoubtedly astrologers, forerunners of astronomers, connected the exploding star with the birth of the great new king who was to be born.

There is as much evidence for the Star of Bethlehem as there is that Caesar was assassinated, that Napoleon attempted an invasion of Russia, or that the Spanish Armada set sail for the British Isles.

The Feeding of the Five Thousand

What shall we say about the multiplying of the loaves and fishes as described by Matthew? The account reads as follows:

Jesus . . . withdrew . . . in a boat to a lonely place apart. But when the crowds heard it, they followed him on foot from the towns. As he went ashore he saw a great throng; and he had compassion on them, and healed their sick. When it was evening the disciples came to him and said, "This is a lonely place, and the day is now over; send the crowds away to go into the villages and buy food for themselves." Jesus said, "They need not go away; you give them something to eat." They said to him, "We have only five loaves and two fish." And he said, "Bring them here to me." Then he ordered the crowds to sit down on the grass; and taking the five loaves and the two fish he looked up to heaven, and blessed, and broke and gave the loaves to the disciples, and the disciples gave them to the crowds. And they all ate and were satisfied. And they took up twelve baskets full of the broken pieces left over. And those who ate were about five thousand men, besides women and children. (Matt. 14:13-21)

The believer says, "It's in the Bible; I believe it." The skeptic replies, "Maybe Jesus healed a lot of people of their psychosomatic illnesses, but this feeding a horde of people with two small fish and five loaves of bread is ridiculous. How does anyone go about multiplying the atoms in bread and fish? It's never been done."

What the skeptic means, of course, is that he has never seen it done; nor have I, but just because I do not know how something is accomplished is no basis for disbelief. I cannot for the life of me understand how several thousand bits of information can be placed on a tiny silicone chip and used in a computer to spew out, at blinding speed, tens of thousands of pieces of information, but it is commonplace in the computer industry.

A Sunday school teacher was trying to explain the feeding of the multitude to his class of boys. He said, "Of course, we understand that Jesus didn't actually multiply the bread and fish and feed all those people. What he did was to break the bread of truth to them, and they were all spiritually fed."

One thoughtful boy shot up his hand.

"Yes, Jimmy?"

"Well, if that's so, what was all that stuff they gathered up in the baskets afterwards?" Good question.

All four of the Gospel writers record the same event, using slightly different wording. But all the accounts give the same details. John adds the fact that they were barley loaves.

Physicists tell us that matter is composed of atoms, molecules, and, at the core, neutrons and protons which are positively and negatively charged particles of energy. So, matter is simply another manifestation of energy.

John tells us that Jesus "created everything there is—nothing exists that he didn't make" (John 1:3 TLB).

If Jesus was indeed the active force in creation, one assumes that his using energy to transform electrons into matter—bread and fish—would be a relatively minor matter.

Almost inconceivably this event seems to have been banished temporarily from their minds, for later, with a crowd numbering four thousand, Jesus suggested that they should be fed. The disciples asked where, in such a desert, they could find food enough to feed such a horde of people. Without rebuking them for their failure to recall how he had once before fed a vast throng, he simply asked how many loaves they had.

Jesus repeated the "miracle" on this occasion. The only food available was seven loaves and a few small fish. The crowd was fed, and seven baskets of food were filled afterward.

What About Demon-Possession?

The commonly accepted explanation of the "casting out of demons" is that people who were supposedly demon-possessed were either insane persons or epileptics. Everyone knows, it is argued, that there is no such thing as an actual demon. Translations: "I have never encountered one, therefore I cannot believe they exist."

The simplest solution is to assume that so-called demon-possession is simply a manifestation of emotional illness; that Jesus accommodated his language—when speaking of demons—to the understanding of the uneducated people of his day. But there is some evidence that needs to be examined.

Within the past few decades the Roman Catholic Church has emerged from the Middle Ages into the twentieth century, and is in the process of discarding a number of ancient encrustations. However, one concept which they still hold has to do with demon-possession. They have a prescribed service of exorcism in which certain priests, trained for this activity, are permitted to perform.

More convincing to my mind is the experience of a very realistic, down-to-earth friend of mine, the Reverend Jim Reid. He is the chaplain to the Las Vegas Strip. Jim has written, with convincing humility and openness, about some of his experiences in Las Vegas, which can easily change one's mind about demon-possession.

A minister who had become something of an expert on the cults and the occult conducted a seminar on the subject at a Las Vegas church some years ago. He spoke of witchcraft, white and black magic, Satanism and demonology. Jim Reid was in attendance. A minister called him several months later and told him that he had a young man in his church who believed himself to be possessed and asked him to assist in an exorcism. Jim replied that he had studied the subject thoroughly, but felt quite unqualified to perform an exorcism. However, he agreed to make an attempt. The minister brought the young man to Jim's office a few nights later.

The victim told Jim that he had become involved in the occult when he was a sophomore in high school. The young man said:

"I was assigned to write a paper on Satan worship and witchcraft in the Middle Ages. I was supposed to compare it with present-day practices. I did the research on the Middle Ages and became fascinated by it. Since I was living in Springfield, Missouri, at the time—where there is a Church of Satan—I began attending the services to gather more information. Before long, I was doing the chants and calling up Omar. . . .

"Omar was my spirit 'friend.' He could give me just about anything I wanted. I had sex with an endless string of girls whom Omar provided for me. He gave me lots of other things as well.

"However, one day I seemed to wake up to what was happening to me. I knew I didn't want to marry any of these girls whom Omar gave me, and for sure I didn't want to be married in the Church of Satan. I had attended a satanic wedding. The bride was fifteen. After the vows were said, she lay nude on the altar while thirteen men had sex with her before her husband did. I didn't want anything like that for my wife-to-be."

He tried to break away, but reported that Omar wouldn't let him go. "Every night he comes to me in my sleep and I often wake up screaming."

Jim Reid, trying to recall all that Derek Prince and Kurt Koch had written on the subject, began.

The Exorcism

After praying for protection for all in the house, he called on the young man to repeat after him:

"Lord, I have called on the powers of darkness. I have worshiped the devil. Forgive me. I now surrender all my life without reservation to Jesus Christ as my Savior and Lord. Come into my life, Lord Jesus, and take complete control. I now renounce the devil. I now renounce all the powers of darkness. I now renounce Omar."

To this point, he was able to repeat each line as I uttered it, but when he tried to renounce Omar he began to gag.

"I renounce O-O-Omar." He managed to get it out. . . .

When I finished praying I said, "Omar, in Jesus' name, I command you to leave this young man. Go where Jesus sends you."

The man's body began to twitch. I repeated my command: "Omar, in Jesus' name, I command you to leave this young man. Go where Jesus sends you."

With this the victim's body became rigid. He let out a scream, then collapsed unconscious.

Jim and his friend thought the exorcism was over, but they were wrong. After talking for an hour or so with them, the young man fell to the floor unconscious.

I prayed some more . . . . Then, "In Jesus' name I command you to come out of this boy."

A demon answered, "This is *my* body!"

I responded, "It's not your body any longer; it belongs to the Lord Jesus. You must leave."

He screamed and left. . . .

Another spoke, "I'll leave. But I'm going to do one thing. I'm going to kill this boy within ten days."

"No, you're not," I answered. "You no longer have

authority over this young man. He belongs to Jesus. You must leave."

Suddenly the man began to strangle himself with his own hands. During this contest with the demons Randy arrived and was assisting me. . . .

The man raised up on all fours, lifting Randy, Bob, and me with him. He let out another scream.

The demon was gone. The man collapsed again. . . .

As each of the spirits left, we could feel certain muscles relax, but still many were tense. Then the young man stuck out his tongue farther than I have ever seen a human tongue extended. He curled it like a snake and clawed at the couch and floor with his hands.

"In Jesus' name I command you to leave this man."

This time there was a hissing sound and some more muscles relaxed.

Again and again I repeated the formula, "In Jesus' name . . ." Again and again the young man gagged, coughed, wheezed, and screamed, and with each oral release we felt muscles relax.

Finally the last spirit cried, "He's only a boy! he's only a boy! he's only a boy!" With each phrase his voice got higher; then he let out a scream and was gone. Immediately the young man opened his eyes and asked, "What's going on?" (*Praising God on the Las Vegas Strip* by Jim Reid)

That was the end of the possession.

The New Testament records at least eighteen instances of Jesus exorcising demons. If Jesus, in calling these people demon-possessed, simply accommodated himself to the superstitious beliefs of the people, it would appear to be the only instance in which he refused to call things by their right names. It does not seem to fit Jesus' personality to alter his practice of complete honesty and openness, in order to go along with a current belief in the idea of demon-possession.

It needs to be borne in mind that in supposed cases of demon-possession in modern times, the victims appear to have been dabbling in the occult, or openly committed to the worship of Satan.

The issue will not be decided in the near future. Believers in the New Testament as an all-sufficient guide for faith and practice will go on believing that Jesus cast out demons and that casting out demons probably happens today. Doubters will have their own views. It will not be resolved by debate.

We have a right to look at such phenomena with a certain amount of skepticism. The naïve are easily deceived, and deceived once too often, become legitimately cautious about believing anything.

Raising the Dead

There is no conceivable way of demonstrating beyond all doubt that *any* historical event of raising the dead actually occurred, unless there exists irrefutable physical evidence that it happened. For instance, the pyramids of Egypt, of Mexico, and of Tikal in Guatemala, are actual proof that unnamed persons labored on those magnificent structures. But without visible proof we are left to our own resources: we either believe that Caesar lived, or label it a myth; that Cyrus was a mighty monarch, or that historians lied.

This is also true with the account of Jesus' raising of the dead. Three instances are recorded: Jairus' daughter, who had just died; the son of a widow of Nain; and Lazarus, who was dead for four days. Either these incidents happened, or Mark, Luke, and John lied about them or, to be more charitable, they were misled or misinformed, or in the case of Mark, who claimed to have been present, that he imagined it.

Mark records the restoration to life of Jairus' daughter (Mark 5:22-43). Luke gives us an account of the raising from the dead of the son of a widow, who was even then following the funeral procession to the cemetery (Luke 7:11-17).

We might suppose it possible that in both instances it was a case of suspended animation; that Jesus with his keen perception, realized this and revived them. It becomes difficult to sustain this idea when we come to the raising of Lazarus, who had been dead four days, bound hand and foot with grave clothes (John 11:38-44). Jesus' resurrection is dealt with later.

The ability to believe is both an intellectual and an emotional process. I have dealt in counseling sessions with scores of persons who, as children, were so badly deceived and disappointed by their parents that they had become cynical doubters. If a child, who needs love and affirmation, is denied this fundamental need and if promises are made and then broken, is it surprising that he or she becomes a skeptic, hesitant to believe in love, in God, in miracles?

Deep skepticism is born, not in the mind, but in the heart of an unloved, deceived child. It is not intellectual doubt, but emotional deprivation that is at the root. The child of broken promises and failed hopes may want to believe, but cannot, until the warmth of love melts the rusted lock on the door of hope.

God's love, mediated through humans, is the medicine for the healing of hurts, long forgotten but still alive in the inner child of the past. Your greatest gift to another can be the expression of that redemptive, unconditional love.

8

Jesus' Death and Atonement

His atoning death is the ultimate demonstration of God's infinite love.

—C. Gillette

I was having lunch with a very perceptive minister friend who had been a pastor and Bible student for many years. I asked, "Do you understand the atonement?"

He did not bother to go into all of the theories of the atonement, with which we were both familiar; but with disarming simplicity he shared his profound belief in an event he could not fully understand. Who can comprehend infinite redemptive love?

On another occasion I was seated in a church, sharing in the congregational singing of "How Great Thou Art." My gaze fastened on the large cross facing the congregation. It was a singularly beautiful cross, faced with gold and illumined from behind. As I sang the words of the hymn some powerful feelings surged up within me, which translated into such words as *beautiful! awesome! wonderful! beyond comprehension!* There was beauty in the knowledge that God sent his Son into the world to identify with us; and in the awareness that Jesus was willing to die for us. It is terrible to contemplate the physical agony he experienced, the emotional and spiritual pain he must have suffered as he felt the rejection of his own people whom he came to save, and the abandonment by his disciples.

It is wonderful to realize that Jesus was enacting—demonstrating, if you will—the infinite and unconditional love of God. It is as much beyond my human comprehension as is the concept that space is infinite.

Did Jesus Die in Despair or Triumph?

There is a fascinating truth about the crucifixion which has eluded Christian theologians. It has been pointed out by a Jewish psychologist and author, Erich Fromm. This great truth has not yet been fully recognized by biblical scholars.

Erich Fromm presents this neglected fact:

Psalm 22 has played a decisive role in the story of the crucifixion of Jesus. Matthew 27:46 reports: "And about the ninth hour Jesus cried with a loud voice, 'Eli, Eli, lama sabachthani?' that is, 'My God, my God, why hast thou forsaken me?' "

It is an almost unbelievable idea that Jesus should have died with words that expressed utter despair. This has, of course, been noted by many interpreters of the Gospel, who explain the apparent absurdity by pointing to the fact that Jesus was God and man, and as man he died in despair. This explanation is not very satisfactory. There have been many human martyrs, before and after Jesus, who died in full faith and showing no trace of despair . . . .

The answer to this puzzling question seems to be simple. In the Jewish tradition up to this day, the books of the Pentateuch, the first five books, or weekly portions of it, or some prayers, are cited by the first major word or sentence. In other words, the Gospels tell us that Jesus, when He was dying, recited Psalm 22. The psalm begins in despair, but it ends in an enthusiastic mood of faith and hope. In fact, there is hardly any psalm which would be better suited to the enthusiastic mood of faith and hope . . . than the end of this psalm: "Posterity shall serve him; men shall tell of the Lord to the coming generations; men proclaim his deliverance to a people yet unborn, that he has wrought it." In Hebrew *ki-asah*—that he has done it. (*You Shall Be as Gods*, Fawcett Publications, 1966)

It is unfortunate, as Fromm points out, that Christian scholars were not aware of this Jewish custom of citing a book or chapter in its entirety by quoting its first sentence.

No, Jesus did not die in despair, but in triumph.

How can we define the love of God? If two lovers were to try to analyze their love, something would be lost. A clinically oriented observer, in an effort to analyze the love relationship, might want to check their blood pressure, the hormone output, respiration, pulse rate, and a dozen or two other physiological manifestations. After listing all of these, would we know anything about love other than some clinical facts?

When theologians theorize and agonize over the minutiae of biblical interpretations of the atonement, I cringe. It is not an event that can be captured and defined in lofty phrases, however technically true they may be. Any definition or explanation of the atonement leaves one with a sense of futility.

I knew a young man, reared by an alcoholic father and a series of prostitutes. He was bailed out of the drunk tank at age seventeen, by a Christian worker, and taken in by a group of Christians. Later, he told me, he heard the statement of Tillich, "You are accepted by that which is greater than you. Simply accept the fact that you are accepted. When that happens, you experience grace." At that moment something happened. It helped explain his total, loving acceptance by a Christian group. And at that moment, he became a Christian, and later a minister.

But Tillich's statement is meaningless for some people; love and grace and acceptance and forgiveness must be experienced to be understood. Intellectual understanding of a biblical proposition is an interesting mental process, but does not constitute genuine acceptance at a deep level.

I recall a delightful woman who had never felt any love from her cold and unfeeling parents. She said, "They told me ten thousand times how much they loved me. They showered me with all manner of material possessions, but they never held me, touched me. I got no hugs or other manifestations of affection. So I never *felt* love. To this day I find it difficult to feel much of anything when people try to express love. I can hear what they are saying, but love has to be demonstrated and felt, not just talked about."

Love Must Be Demonstrated

This is why I believe that Jesus enacted on the cross the full measure of divine love, as a demonstration of the infinite love God has always felt for his children.

The news media recently carried the story of a fire that broke out in a home during the night. The father and mother each gathered up a small child and hurried out of the flaming house. The father then rushed back into the blazing inferno to rescue a third

[122]

child, still in an upstairs room. He fought his way through the billowing smoke, seized the child, covered her with a blanket, and stumbled back outside. The little girl was saved, but her father died that night of smoke inhalation.

The daughter will spend the rest of her life in the realization that her father died for her. But the love that drove him back into the flaming house had always been there. It was part of his nature, expressed to the uttermost in a night of tragedy.

This analogy, as any human parallel, falls short in illustrating the eternal redemptive love of God, but it does illustrate a truth which is often clouded by a false attempt to make the blood of Christ an active literal agent involved in divine redemption. God has always given redemptive love; the prophets of old expressed it; but Jesus lived it out in a manner that stirs our spiritual and emotional natures, as no verbal statement could possibly do.

About 400 B.C. God spoke through Malachi:

"I am the Lord—I do not change. That is why you are not already utterly destroyed [for my mercy endures forever].

"Though you have scorned my laws from earliest times, yet you may still return to me," says the Lord of Hosts. "Come and I will forgive you!" (Mal. 3:6-7*a* TLB)

Here God extends forgiveness and pardon four hundred years before Christ. Divine pardon and acceptance, then, did not begin when Christ died on the cross; but that event dramatized the eternal, unchanging love of God. It grips our attention, inspires devotion and repentance and love; it does something to our emotions.

The statement, "The blood of Jesus, his Son,

cleanses us from all sin," cannot be taken literally. How can blood shed two thousand years ago affect one today? And if it did, how would it do so? This is a beautiful figurative statement which was never meant to be forced into some rigid, literal theological concept. Jesus acting out the infinite love of the Father and forgiving his enemies while on the cross touches us and tells us something about the love of God which no verbal assurance could ever do.

The message of the cross is that God is and has always been ready to extend forgiveness; that he cares for us as a loving parent cares for his child, only to an infinite degree.

Did Jesus die for humankind? Yes, of course, he did! He died in order that we might grasp at the very depth of our natures some fragment of the infinitude of his loving concern for us. To believe in Jesus is to believe that God is like him, filled with tender compassion, anxious to accept and forgive all who come in sincere repentance.

Susan Atkins was one of the Manson family of murderers. Convicted of murder and imprisoned in the California Institute for Women awaiting execution, Susan was visited briefly by a Roman Catholic priest who handed her a Bible sent to her by a woman named Horvath. Susan tossed it carelessly into a box in the corner of her cell.

Later, she picked up the Bible and opened it to the flyleaf on which was this message, "Jesus, my prayer is that you reveal yourself to Susan Atkins." Susan thought, "Here I was, waiting to die, . . . and now, a Bible from some weird little old lady!"

As she dwelt on her wretched condition, she was consumed by guilt and loneliness. Even her body was deteriorating badly. Drugs and an inadequate diet had played havoc with her teeth, and she was a physical wreck.

Sitting on her bunk, she was startled to hear a news broadcast announcing that the death penalty in California had been abolished. She wasn't going to be executed! Describing her reaction to the news, she said:

Almost unconsciously, I felt myself slipping off my bed toward the floor. I was on my knees. And the tears came. In seconds, sobs were rising from deep in my chest, and I was weeping audibly, not loudly, but openly. And for the first time since my mother's death, I spoke to God. I remember distinctly; I called him "God," not "Father" or "Lord." It was only two short sentences: "Thanks, God. I want to thank you for letting me live—and all the others, too."

One night sometime later she had a dream in which

masses of people filled the room. It was a sea of people. They picked me up over their heads and started walking with me, carrying me somehow out of the big room, out into the open.

There in the open space—wide and colorful, clean and pure—was something, a being. . . . "That must be God," I heard myself saying. . . .

The being then walked over and tapped me on the head—right on top of my head. He was larger than I had realized. He looked into my face and said: "The trouble with you is your indifference to me. I want you to think about your indifference."

I was instantly awake. My heart was in my throat, and I felt I might choke. Perspiration covered my body, but nonetheless I felt chilly. I was afraid and cold.

On another occasion when she was thinking about giving her life to Jesus Christ she heard:

"Behold, I stand at the door, and knock. . . ." Did I hear someone say that? I don't know. But the statement was there. All else stood still.

"Okay. If you're there, come on in."

Total stillness . . . and then: "All right. I'll come in, but you must open the door. . . ."

Suddenly as though on a movie screen, there in my thoughts was a door. It had a handle. I took hold of it, and pulled. It opened.

The whitest, most brilliant light I had ever seen poured over me. I was standing in darkness, but the light pushed the darkness completely out of sight. It vanished behind me. There was only light. And in the center of the flood of brightness was an even brighter light. Vaguely, there was the form of a man. I knew it was Jesus.

He spoke to me—literally, plainly, matter-of-factly spoke to me in my nine-by-eleven prison cell: "Susan, I am really here. I'm really coming into your heart to stay. Right now you are being born again and you will live with me in heaven through all eternity, forever and ever. This is really happening. It is not a dream. You are now a child of God. You are washed clean and your sins have all been forgiven. . . ."

For the first time in my memory I felt clean, fully clean, inside and out. In twenty-six years I had never been so happy. (*Child of Satan, Child of God* by Susan Atkins with Bob Slosser, Logos International, 1977)

Susan was later baptized in a tank outside the main building, and was joyously welcomed into the family of God. The experience of God's love in Jesus Christ, not theories of the atonement, had changed her life.

9

Death and the Resurrection

I am vitally interested in the future, because I intend to spend the rest of my life there.

—*Charles F. Kettering*

Did Jesus literally rise from the dead, or, as some maintain, was it simply mass hallucination, the product of wishful thinking born of despair?

I have a minister friend, a splendid person in every respect, who believes that the resurrection accounts are an effort to explain that the message of Jesus is immortal, and that his spirit lives on.

It is rather anomalous that a Christian minister denies the reality of the resurrection, while a Jewish scholar believes that Jesus literally rose from the dead.

Pinchas Lapide, an Orthodox Jewish scholar, and a professor at German's Göttingen University, writes, "I would not exclude such a resurrection as within the range of possibility." In his book, *Resurrection—A Jewish Faith Experience*, Lapide argues that

the Christian church must somehow be part of God's plan. If the two religions [Judaism and Christianity] both derive from the same God, . . . Christianity could not be founded upon a lie. And since it "stands or falls" with the Easter

[127]

story, . . . the church was "born out of an act of the will of God, which the New Testament authors call the Resurrection of Jesus from the dead." . . .

He notes that . . . more than 500 Jews . . . saw the resurrected Jesus. . . . Lapide argues, "if the Disciples were totally disappointed and on the verge of desperate flight because of the very real reason of the Crucifixion, it took another very real reason in order to transform them from a band of disheartened and dejected Jews into the most self-confident missionary society in world history."

Lapide . . . has been known to twit German liberal Christians about their lack of faith. The demythologizers of Easter, he says, are "sawing off the branch of faith upon which they are sitting." (*Time*, May 7, 1979)

This provides us with the anomalous situation of an Orthodox Jew criticizing Christian leaders for their failure to accept the resurrection as a literal fact.

There is a seldom-discussed tantalizing mystery concerning Jesus' physical appearance being changed in some manner after his resurrection. The two disciples who met him on the road to Emmaus did not recognize him, until some familiar gesture in the breaking of the bread alerted them to the fact that it was Jesus who was in their presence.

After the resurrection the disciples spent the night fishing, without results. "Just as day was breaking, Jesus stood on the beach; yet the disciples did not know that it was Jesus. Jesus said to them, 'Children, have you any fish?' " (John 21:4-5). "No," they said. He told them to cast their net on the right side of the boat. When they did so, they were unable to draw in the net because of the large school of fish the net enclosed. When they finally dragged the net ashore,

Jesus had a fire going, and said, "Come and have breakfast."

We read, "Now none of the disciples dared ask him, 'Who are you?' They knew it was the Lord" (John 21:12). There was apparently some significant physical change in his appearance.

Thomas, in the upper room, found Jesus' physical appearance so changed that he could not believe until he had seen the nail prints and the wounded side.

The apostle Paul tells us: "When he comes back he will take these dying bodies of ours and change them into glorious bodies like his own, using the same mighty power that he will use to conquer all else everywhere" (Phil. 3:21 TLB). Apparently his resurrection body was glorious, and our resurrected forms will be changed in the same manner. (Thank God for that!)

Along with the mystery of the incarnation, the Trinity, and the problem of sin, suffering, and sorrow, we now have the mystery of the transformed body of Jesus, who at first was not recognized even by his disciples.

What About the Future Life?

Millions long for immortality who don't know what to do with themselves on a rainy Sunday afternoon, but not everyone believes in life after death.

The Gallup Poll provides us with some interesting figures based on personal interviews with over 10,000 persons in sixty nations. People were asked the question, "Do you believe in life after death?"

Here are the results of the Poll:

India	81%	Italy	46%
United States	69%	United Kingdom	43%
Canada	54%	France	38%
Australia	48%	West Germany	33%
		Japan	18%

India is the only nation with a higher percentage than the U.S. The people there believe in reincarnation and transmigration (the rebirth of a human soul in various animals as well as persons).

Some people seem to have an excessive preoccupation with the "furniture of heaven, and the temperature of hell." Such an inordinate interest, to the exclusion of one's current here-and-now life situation could be considered neurotic. But Jesus had so much to say about eternal life that surely it behooves us to give some serious thought to it.

We assume that the reason the Bible gives no specific description of heaven is because we could not comprehend it.

Jesus said to the Twelve, "I have yet many things to say to you, but you cannot bear them now" (John 16:12). They could not have understood it if he had told them some of the mysteries yet to be unfolded, any more than most of us can understand the implications of Einstein's equation $E = MC^2$. That equation is meaningless to me, but implicit in it for a physicist are the mysteries of time and space. When Einstein says that time and space are curved, I don't know what he is talking about. So, Jesus must have found it impossible to convey to human minds the details of what we are to experience in heaven. In the Book of Revelation, John gives us some figurative pictures to try and put into words what cannot be expressed about heaven.

A significant number of people declared clinically dead have returned to relate their experience. After interviewing several hundred of them, psychiatrist Raymond A. Moody wrote about their experiences in his book *Life After Life*. Their accounts are remarkably similar, though each expressed it differently. One said:

I heard the doctors say that I was dead, and that's when I began to feel as though I was tumbling, actually kind of floating, through this blackness, which was some kind of enclosure. There are not really words to describe this. Everything was very black, except that way off from me, I could see this light. It was a very, very brilliant light, but not too large at first. It grew larger as I came nearer to it.

I was trying to get to that light at the end, because I felt that it was Christ, and I was trying to reach that point. It was not a frightening experience. It was more or less a pleasant thing. For immediately, being a Christian, I had connected the light with Christ, who said, "I am the light of the world." I said to myself, "If this is it, if I am to die, then I know who waits for me at the end, there in that light."

Another person reported:

I got up from the bed and walked into the hall to get a drink, and it was at that point, as they found out later, that my appendix ruptured. I became very weak, and I fell down. I began to feel a sort of drifting, a movement of my real being in and out of my body, and to hear beautiful music. I floated on down the hall and out the door. . . . Then I floated right straight on through the screen, just as though it weren't there, and up into this pure crystal clear light, an illuminating white light. It was beautiful and so bright, so radiant, but it didn't hurt my eyes. It's not any kind of light you can describe on earth. I didn't actually see a person in this light, and yet it has a special identity. . . . It is a light of perfect understanding and perfect love.

The thought came to my mind, "Lovest thou me?" This was not exactly in the form of a question, but I guess the connotation of what the light said was, "If you do love me, go back and complete what you began in your life.

Some of the people reported that they could see their own bodies below as they floated above them. Some experienced a "review" of their lives. There seemed to be no sense of judgment from the being as the events were being reviewed.* Dr. Moody writes:

The remembrance was instantaneous; everything appeared at once, and they could take it all in with one mental glance. . . .

Yet, despite its rapidity, my informants agree that the review, almost always described as a display of visual imagery, is incredibly vivid and real. In some cases, the images are reported to be in vibrant color, three-dimensional, and even moving. And even if they are flicking rapidly by, each image is perceived and recognized. . . .

Some of those I interviewed claimed that . . . everything they had ever done was there in this review—from the most insignificant to the most meaningful. Others explain that what they saw was mainly the highlights of their lives. . . .

Some people characterize this as an educational effort on the part of the being of light. As they witness the display, the being seems to stress the importance of two things in life: Learning to love other people and acquiring knowledge.

The Bible speaks of rewards and conveys the idea of punishment. But in one sense, there is neither divine

---

*A few people who "died" and returned reported hell-like experiences. One who appeared on national television described his terror and said that he now reads his Bible and prays daily.

punishment nor rewards either in this life or the next. There are only *consequences*. God is not punitive, nor does he hand out rewards. Heaven is not a reward, but the inevitable, natural abode of the redeemed. Hell is not a punishment, but the only other place in the universe where spiritual rejects can go. The rejects are not being punished, but having rejected Christ, they experience the inevitable result. Heaven and hell are both consequences, the result of decisions made in this life.

If one lives his life in violation of known laws of health and physical well-being, he is "living in sin," in that he is violating some universal principles to his own destruction. God does not punish him, though the consequences of his actions may be sickness, or even death. It may *feel* like punishment, but he is experiencing only the consequences of his mistaken decisions and actions.

In the same way, a person who disregards the teachings of Jesus and willfully pursues a life that violates basic spiritual principles will reap the consequences. He is condemned, not by God, but by his own actions. Everyone, ultimately, sits down to a banquet of consequences.

Death, the Distasteful Subject

We humans, by and large, hate to be reminded of our mortality. For this reason the subject of death is seldom dealt with, except when attendance at a funeral service seems obligatory, or some mention is made of the death of a person whom we know. Other than that, we tend to ignore the subject, as though it will go away if we don't talk about it.

One device for avoiding the fateful subject of death is to conceal our anxiety beneath a façade of humor. Comedian Woody Allen, who, though an atheist, seems preoccupied with the subject of death, said, "I don't want to achieve immortality through my work; I want to achieve it through not dying."

In a comic strip, Officer Casey is talking to Mr. Proust, a funeral director. Casey asks, "How do you handle an atheist's funeral?" Proust replies, "A combo plays Cole Porter favorites, then while I read the Quantum Theory to the assemblage, one of my aides serves cold duck. Then we escort the widow down to the computer mating service."

Another oft-quoted witticism tells us that everyone wants to go to heaven, but nobody wants to die. This conceals a profound truth. We long for the Elysian Fields of glory, but dread the thought of death, and quite rightly so.

In such devious ways we conceal our distaste for confronting the inevitability of death.

Psychology Today conducted a survey in 1979 to discover how its readers felt about death. More than 30,000 readers replied, and 2,000 sent in substantial letters with their replies. An earlier survey dealing with sex drew a total of slightly over 20,000 responses. The editors were surprised that the topic of death and dying created more interest than the subject of sex, by a very substantial margin.

A third of those responding to the poll could not recall the subject of death ever having been mentioned during childhood. Another third recalled that it was mentioned with a measure of discomfort. In only 30 percent of the families was death talked about openly.

The Bible speaks of death as the enemy: "The last enemy to be destroyed is death" (I Cor. 15:26). And in a passage conveying the assurance of Christ's ultimate triumph over evil, we read: "God himself will be with them; he will wipe away every tear from their eyes, and *death shall be no more*, neither shall there be mourning nor crying any more, for the former things have passed away" (Rev. 21:3c-4, italics added).

What Makes One a Christian?

What is it, according to the Bible, that qualifies a person to enter heaven? What does it mean to be "saved"? What makes one a Christian? Is it a quality of life? Doing good? Being a loving person? Believing a given set of doctrines? Having faith? Living the right kind of life? Avoiding evil? Believing in Christ? Being baptized?

John, in the first chapter of his lovely Gospel, puts it very simply: "He [Jesus Christ] came to his own home, and his own people received him not. *But to all who received him, who believed in his name, he gave power to become children of God'* (John 1:11-12, italics added).

Various religious groups define a child of God in different ways. Perhaps there is an element of truth in all of the various definitions; but in essence we can say that a child of God is one who commits all of himself that he is aware of to all of Christ he understands. From this point on there will be many recommitments, numerous failures and false starts, a thousand confessions and new beginnings. A saint has been defined as one who confesses more and more, and sins less and less. This is true of Christian growth.

The Bible tells of a time when all the works of man shall be destroyed, when all civilization will be crumbled to dust, and the works of man will be consumed in the intense heat. When the last remnant of humanity has vanished, every fear-crazed animal has perished in the final holocaust, and all life has ceased, the earth which God created in all its pristine glory will remain.

When all the satellites have completed their final orbits and have crashed to flaming extinction in the sea, when every mountain has been shaken to its foundations and leveled with the plain, when the world becomes an uninhabited cinder and finally, like a flame that has flared and died out, the stars will remain. But in time they too will disintegrate.

As the eons roll on and all the created matter of the universe is drawn back into the vortex and is transmuted into primordial energy, God, who created matter in the first place, will then be ready for another "big bang" such as the one which began the former creation. There remains now one fixed point in the universe: God, the One who said to Moses on Mt. Sinai, "I AM WHO I AM" (Exod. 3:14). The immortal, transcendant I AM remains. But he is not alone.

As the climax of his creative process, God created male and female in his own spiritual image. "And behold it was very good," Genesis tells us. So, what remains is God and his family of children who are spirits, made of the same divine essence as the Father. We are in small what he is in great. We each have a minuscule set of capacities like those possessed by God. His are infinite, our finite.

In the midst of life's joys and sorrows, its struggles and disappointments, victories and defeats, when all the tears have been shed and all of life's fleeting honors have vanished; when even death, the last enemy, has been destroyed, we, the victors remain. There can be no final defeat for us, for God cannot be defeated.

Shall we exist throughout eternity, reposing on fleecy clouds, playing harps or rehearsing with some celestial choir? I think not. All of the best imaginings of man and his most vivid speculations of what heaven is like, must surely be but feeble and absurd guesses.

But we are assured that the redeemed "shall reign forever and ever," and that God "will wipe away every tear from their eyes." This, then, is the final triumph of God and man.

10

What Is Conversion?

He who believes in him is not condemned.
—*John* 3:18a

You have undoubtedly had the experience of standing on the shore of a lake, or the ocean, on a moonlit night. The moon sends a silvery ray of light over the water directly to the place where you stand, as though it existed only for you. As you move, to right or left, the moonlight follows you, wherever you go along the beach. In somewhat the same way, God's forgiveness and love exist for you as if you were the only person on earth. It follows you, seeks you out. You are not compelled to accept the gentle, unrelenting love that is being directed toward you. You have the choice—to ignore it, to think about it momentarily, or to dwell and revel in it. You may have as much of it as you wish. God awaits your response to his divine initiative. And just as each person experiences the moonlight in his or her own way, so each person's experiences of God is different. There are as many kinds of conversion as there are people.

A Persecutor Is Changed

The spectacular conversion of Paul, on the Damascus road, has been described innumerable times in sermons and books. It was a truly dramatic experience.

Having a fanatical hatred for all Christians, Paul was on his way to Damascus to seek out the Christians there and drag them in chains back to Jerusalem.

As he was nearing Damascus on this mission, suddenly a brilliant light from heaven spotted down on him! He fell to the ground and heard a voice saying to him, "Paul! Paul! Why are you persecuting me?"

"Who is speaking, sir?" Paul asked.

And the voice replied, "I am Jesus, the one you are persecuting! Now get up and go into the city and await my further instructions." (Acts 9:3-6 TLB)

The men traveling with Paul heard the voice, but saw no one. When Paul rose from the ground he found he was blind. He remained so until he arrived in Damascus, and a Christian by the name of Ananias laid his hands on him.

Everyone is familiar with this remarkable conversion. It makes good reading, partly because it was so dramatic—a brilliant light, a disembodied voice, and the temporary blindness—and because Paul subsequently became the chief exponent of Christianity and wrote a large part of the New Testament.

An Atheist Becomes a Christian

William J. Murray (his real name) grew up in the home of a fiery, dedicated professional atheist. His mother is Madalyn Murray O'Hair, who has been suing state and federal agencies for many years over such issues as prayer in public schools. Her son, William, joined her some years ago in a suit to declare public prayer in schools to be unconstitutional.

William J. Murray suddenly became a Christian, and now repudiates all of his former views. In a letter to a local newspaper in his home city of Austin, Texas, he wrote:

Looking back on the 33 years of life I wasted without faith and without God, I pray that I may be able to correct some of the wrong I have created. The part I played as a teen-ager in removing prayer from public schools was criminal. I would like to apologize to the people of Austin for the part I played in building the personal empire of Madalyn O'Hair. My efforts to that end were an affront to the people of Austin, the people of the nation and to God. . . . My crime was two-fold in that I was aware of the wrong of my actions at the time, and I continued them for the purpose of financial profit. I was continuing to practice the hateful and anti-moral way of life I had learned from birth in an atheistic home. (*Austin American-Statesman*, May 12, 1980)

This spectacular conversion of a crusading atheist, reared in the home of America's outstanding professional atheist, is most gratifying. His repudiation of his mother's teachings heartens Christians everywhere. It makes good reading, and an excellent sermon illustration.

He Didn't Need AA

Someone told me the story of a friend's conversion. We'll call him Fred. He was a confirmed alcoholic and wife-beater. He was a poor father and had severely alienated every member of his family. Highly successful in business, he devoted all his time to his various enterprises and gave little attention to his family. When he did go home he was usually drunk, and violent scenes often occurred.

One day Fred suddenly asked himself, "What am I doing to my family?" He thought about it at some length and realized that alcohol played a major role in his destructive behavior. He decided then and there never to take another drink. And he didn't. He didn't join Alcoholics Anonymous, yet his cure was permanent. He just stopped cold, something which rarely occurs. He went to church with his wife and soon presented himself for membership on profession of faith. Since then he has been an ideal husband and father. He has a daily quiet time and meets weekly with a group of men for Bible study. His family's prayers were answered.

That makes a good story, and it's true. The one difficulty with it is that most people's conversions seldom happen just that way. Most alcoholics have to attend endless AA meetings in order to achieve sobriety. A great many of them experience occasional lapses before the cure is totally effective.

To hold up Fred's religious experience as an illustration of the power of Christ to transform a person is valid, but it is quite wrong to suggest that anyone else is likely to achieve sobriety and a transformed home life in precisely the same way.

Conversion: Only the First Step

Because a dramatic conversion makes a good story, much more attention is focused on a sudden conversion—from drug addiction, alcoholism, crime, or atheism—than a less spectacular religious experience. This often makes people who grew up in a Christian home and never knew the time when they did not love Christ wonder if they have been genuinely converted because nothing dramatic occurred. Their experience has been a gradual growing faith in Christ.

Very few people have had remarkable religious experiences, but then how many people have been persecuted Christians, atheists, alcoholics, wife-beaters, or members of a murder cult? Most people have a relatively low-key conversion experience. For many, it consists of a gradual or sudden conviction that something is lacking in their lives, that committing themselves to Christ and joining the family of God is the first step toward emotional and spiritual wholeness.

I say the first step, for that is just what it is—the first in a lifelong growth process.

Brent had been converted and was active in his church, but though he considered himself "saved," his religious experience had not saved him from a terrifying anxiety and depression. His emotional symptoms developed some months after his conversion. He was barely able to hold a job and was functioning at about 50 percent of normal.

He wrote a most heartening letter after he completed his therapy at the Burlingame Counseling Center.

I would like to tell you what has happened to me since our first contact two years ago. My life has changed drastically.

Primal Integration definitely pulled me out of the depths of despair. Because of my Primal therapy, I started to function again, and in a short time was functioning quite well.

Then you sent me a letter telling of a Yokefellow group that was starting, and asked if I was interested. I decided to go, though I was quite skeptical.

The group experience has let me become so much freer of guilt. I can't even describe in words how very important that is to me. Man, I'm okay. Down inside me I'm okay!

I now find I'm so much less critical of others. Because I'm okay, they're okay, too. Therefore my relationships with others have changed tremendously.

The group started September 10. On October 1 I started to diet. I weighed 247 pounds. Only twice in my life have I ever been on a diet. Both times I lost 20 pounds, quit and regained the 20 pounds.

This time I have lost 57 pounds, and am positive I will reach my ideal weight of 180 pounds soon. Because of all this, my self-image has improved. I take pride in my dress, and more pride in my home. I just generally feel so much better about myself.

I am leading a successful Yokefellow group now, and am quite excited about it. I find that the areas of my growth are unlimited. What has happened to me has spread to my family and my relationship with my father and mother. I praise God for leading me to you, to Primal Integration, and to Yokefellows!

Brent had been converted, but his severe anxiety and depression were unchanged. It required some intensive therapy in a Christian-oriented counseling center to relieve him of his emotional symptoms. His original conversion did not solve all his problems but it was the beginning of a new life.

In numerous passages the Bible declares that if we

seek God with all of our heart, we will surely find him (Jer. 24:7; 29:13). Some people are seeking love with all their hearts, and not finding it. Millions are pursuing wealth with intensity bordering on fanaticism, and not getting it. A host of people are devoting their lives to the pursuit of fame, or notoriety with varying degrees of success.

But the Bible makes the flat statement that when we seek God with all of our hearts, we will find him, and his blessings. Just why should it be so hard? If you want groceries, you go to the market. There is no struggle, no focusing all of one's energies on the goal of buying food. If you want an education, you simply attend a college, or sign up for a night class. But for many people to find God it seems to require the bringing of all of one's attention to a fine point—to want him above all else. Why is this?

I am sure it is not because God hides himself, as Job suggested in a moment of despair. It is rather because we are obtuse, much wedded to the flesh; and God is spirit, who must be worshiped "in spirit and in truth," as Jesus said.

The struggle to hold a job, raise a family, set aside something for the future, and acquire some of the desirable creature comforts are all worthy goals. But they consume such a large part of our time and energy that there is precious little left over for the pursuit of God. The developing of our spiritual lives is usually a poor third, or fifth, or tenth on our list of priorities.

And if things are going reasonably well, there seems no point in becoming a religious fanatic, rushing off to church every time the doors open. There will always be time for that later on, we tell ourselves.

Then something happens.

One seldom makes any important change in personality or life situation except as the result of a deep sense of urgency. This may be the sharp stab of a crisis, the dull throb of frustration, or the deep awareness that something significant is lacking in one's life. In one sense, then, we should thank God for a crisis, or for any threat to our serenity which makes us receptive to the love of God.

I was interrupted by a long distance phone call just now. A man from another state described his problem. He and his wife had separated. He said that he had to make some radical changes in his life or she would divorce him. Even now, he said, it might be too late. He had been seeing a marriage counselor and had discovered that his partly buried hostility toward his father was unconsciously being directed at his wife. "I know this in my head. Now what can I do about it?" he asked.

I explained that his was not a marital problem, but a personality malfunction. He had been reading a book of mine that described Primal Integration, a process of going back into one's childhood and reliving those primal traumas, discharging the anxiety and anger encapsulating them. He asked if he needed that kind of therapy.

I told him that if he could find a quicker, cheaper solution to try it. If not, to come and spend three weeks with us, as hundreds of other hurting people have done. As of now, he is being put on a fairly long waiting list.

If before his wife had asked him to leave, someone had urged him to examine his motivation and go back into his childhood to see how it was destroying his marriage, he would undoubtedly have rejected the

[145]

idea. There was insufficient pain to motivate him. But now there is the very real threat to his marriage. He loves his wife, and rather than lose her he is willing to do whatever is necessary to save the marriage. Pain is a powerful motivator.

Learning to Forgive Ourselves

Ruth Carter Stapleton, who has a national ministry, points out that becoming a Christian does not automatically bring instant happiness and peace. Even the baptism of the Holy Spirit, felt by many to be an added gift, does not always rid one of severe anxiety or depression. Nor, for that matter, does it necessarily provide one with instant self-forgiveness.

A woman who read *The Art of Becoming a Whole Person* wrote me to ask how she could get rid of her self-hate, anxiety, and other personality hang-ups. I referred her to the Pacific Northwest Yokefellow Center in Seattle. The staff there had taken Primal Integration training at our Center. I assured her that they could help her.

She wrote some months later:

When I felt safe and began to trust them, a lot of garbage and hate came up out of me, from my inner self. (There's more to come.) I had crammed it down into my unconscious mind. The real love of the Christian therapists there began to have an effect on me, and I even surprised myself at how honest I was willing to be.

Thanks in part to your book, and the guidance and love of Ted and Chuck and the others at the Pacific Northwest Yokefellow Center, I am becoming real, and true to myself, and to God. I thank God for the books, and for them.

I know now that the guilt and shame and hate don't have

to control my life any longer. The pain of reliving my past does hurt, but with God's grace I am accepting that part of me as well as the good that is in me. It feels good to be real, and not masking myself. The future is going to be real. I am honest with God and with myself and others. I now realize that God can use my past for good. *I have felt forgiveness for the first time in my life!* What a great feeling. The more I understand and accept the real person I am, the more real peace, love, and joy I experience in my life.

I found one of her statements to be very significant: for the first time, "I have *felt* forgiveness." This is the key to the other dividends she is enjoying—peace, love, and joy.

It is not easy to accept divine forgiveness at a deep feeling level. I am convinced that we are able to accept God's forgiveness only *to the extent that we are able to forgive ourselves.* And those of us who were reared in a legalistic or judgmental environment usually tend to have a severely punitive conscience. The lovely young woman who wrote of her experience was able to accept God's full forgiveness only when she undertook Primal Integration and was enabled to discharge the hurts, fear, and anger that had so severely damaged her spiritual life.

One reason we do not seek God with more earnestness is because we are not sufficiently motivated. Another reason is pointed out with great insight by Dr. Vernon Grounds, recently retired president of the Conservative Baptist Theological Seminary in Denver, Colorado. He writes:

Will any honest evangelical deny that the gospel is sometimes misinterpreted? Again and again sermons present the good news of redemption and release as gloomy, morbid, world-denying, puritanical, and re-pressive. God is frequently portrayed not as he really is, the God of Abraham, Isaac and Jacob, the covenant-keeping God and Father of Jesus Christ, the God of wisdom, power, righteousness, love and grace. He is portrayed instead as a sadistic monster, a legalistic tyrant, a cosmic egotist obsessed with minutiae and taboos. It is no wonder, then, that the adherents of a misinterpreted Christianity fail to enjoy a large measure of psychic health.

Let us admit, too, that a discouragingly large percentage of rank-and-file evangelicals are characterized by conflict, tension, fear, guilt, scrupulosity, and aggressiveness. (*Emotional Problems and the Gospel*, Zondervan, 1976)

Such Christians as he describes are poor witnesses to a dynamic religious faith. "If Christians are like that," people are prone to say, "I'd rather not be one."

Growing—The Positive Side

Jeanie Miley, in a splendid little book titled, *Spread Wide the Curtain* (Broadman Press, 1979), tells of her spiritual journey. Jeanie was a nominal Christian, a complainer who made herself unhappy while making mountains out of molehills. A gentle, probing question of a loving friend started her on the quest for wholeness and inner peace. Conversion for Jeanie was not a onetime thing, but a growth process, as it is for many who cannot name the precise day when they made a specific commitment to Christ. Jeanie writes:

It never occurred to me to look within myself to find the source of my alienation and frustration. All I could see, in my acute myopia, were externals that were out of whack. I was bound by the "if only's"—"If only my husband didn't have to be gone so much," "If only I had more money," "If only so-and-so would shape up," or "If only my husband would communicate with me!" . . . I was stuck like a needle on a broken record. . . .

It took a friend who loved me enough to confront me, to be honest with me and to communicate acceptance, love, and grace to bring me to awareness of the sin that was within me. One day, in a moment of weakness, I complained to her, unloading a barrage of trivia . . . she listened quietly, letting me talk. I will never forget her face or her gentle voice as she embraced me and said, "Let me know when you're ready to work on yourself."

This casual comment startled her into action. Already a Christian, now that she saw the need to begin working on herself, she started a program of spiritual growth that was thrilling.

With the support of this friend, my husband Martus, and a loving group of seekers like myself, I began soul searching, a deep, introspection and re-evaluation that has been both excruciatingly painful and painfully exciting. . . .

I began to read countless books on practical Christianity psychology and theology, marriage, child-rearing, and personal growth. My thirst was insatiable, my hunger was all-consuming. One book led me to three more and I was ecstatic about all the new things I was learning. Contact with God and his truths became *the most important goal in my life, and I gave myself totally to this pursuit."* [Emphasis added]

The path was not always easy. She tells how she was invited, with her husband, to attend a Yokefellow group. She went with great reluctance, only because her husband wanted her to attend. In the first few sessions she refused to participate, to open herself up to a "bunch of strangers." She questioned the leader's credentials and discounted the entire process.

But one evening, after months of anxiety over her child, she broke down and wept. There was such overwhelming love and acceptance that she was forever converted to the group process used by Yokefellows. (Later she and her husband led several such groups.)

Jeanie writes: "Salvation, I have learned, is both an event and process, and eternal life has as much to do with the quality of life as with the length of it. Eternal life is knowing God, and I know now that knowing the facts about God and knowing him personally, intimately, daily are two different things altogether."

Philip Yancey writes of his conversion while he was in college. A self-confessed naturalist who did not believe in God, he regarded the activities of his fellow-Christians with deep cynicism. He did all he could to demolish their simplistic faith in God. Then a strange thing happened: "It would have been humiliating and embarrassing had it not been so overwhelmingly delightful. I became a Christian. God met me in an amazing, undeniable way, at a time when I wasn't even looking for him—in fact, while I was denying him. I experienced a true Christian conversion. During a routine (required) prayer meeting with friends, God made contact with me. He showed me his love and forgiveness and I was born again."

Philip then sought ways to explain this sudden transformation to his non-Christian friends.

I tried to think of ways to persuade my friends that I had not gone loony, but rather had found a deeper reality. I knew they wouldn't be attracted to the Christians I knew—I had mocked them too successfully. The idea of miracles came to me. Could I find some absolutely unexplainable miracle? Surely that would prove God's reality.

Why wasn't God more obvious? I wanted him to conduct well-orchestrated televised miracles so that I could invite my skeptical friends to see an act of God they could never deny. . . . What we really need, I thought, is a giant, world-wide awesome display of God's power.

Even as I thought of it, I realized it wouldn't work. The Bible records scores of instances when God really shocked the world. The ten plagues of Egypt, for example. Cecil B. De Mille spent millions to imitate them, and his film sequences still look phony. What of the resurrection of Jesus? More than five hundred people attested that he had come back from the dead, but most people refused to believe them. God himself walked the earth for thirty-three years, teaching and performing astounding miracles. Yet, of those who heard him, only a minority believed. . . .

I don't need miracles to believe; God has lovingly proved himself to me. It only bothers me when I think about my skeptical friends. If God really did a miracle right in front of their eyes, would they believe? I don't know. . . . Some came to believe, some didn't. (Philip Yancey and Tim Stafford, *Unhappy Secrets of the Christian Life*, Zondervan, 1979).

"The Wind Blows Where It Wills"

People come to Christ in a variety of ways. There are as many ways as there are temperaments. God is not limited to express his love in any one particular fashion.

The intellectual may need to understand many things with his mind. Spontaneous, outgoing people are more apt to respond, as did Simon Peter, with less intellectual probing. There are the skeptics, who as children learned not to trust people or God or life without a vast amount of proof. Such people usually suffered so many disappointments that it became difficult for them to trust readily. There are a thousand varieties of people, and Christ stands ready to meet each of them at the point of their need. He waits at the end of all paths. He lures you, with his gentle love, to take still another step in the direction of a whole-hearted commitment to him.

More than the joyous bells of Christmas, or the triumphant anthems we hear at Easter, I am affected by Good Friday. And at any time of the year, when I think of Christ, my mind goes inevitably to the cross, and I am humbled by what happened there. Something beyond intellectual comprehension occurred; it can be *felt* better than explained.

In a Sunday school room in our church was a large picture of Jesus in a lovely garden, surrounded by several children. It was not great art, but it portrayed a great message. One lovely little girl, seated on Jesus' lap, was pointing to his hand. Looking up into his face she was asking, with childlike openness, "What happened to your hand?" I have given up trying to answer that question. It is as great a mystery as the incarnation or the resurrection. It involves infinite redemptive love, for which there is no adequate definition. Words are not capable of describing it without limiting it. Divine love must be experienced, not defined.

No one has ever been loved enough. Nor is anyone capable of giving unconditional love all the time— except Christ. He is the answer to that vague disquietude deep within each of us, for which there is no word. And ultimately there is no answer to be found except in him.

11

Is the Bible Infallible?

It is often supposed that when people stop believing in God they will believe in nothing. Alas, it is worse than that. When they stop believing in God, they believe in anything.

—Malcolm Muggeridge

There was a famous story some years ago, emanating from the office of a computer manufacturer, to the effect that a new model—not fully perfected—was designed to translate from one language into another. One computer wrote out the statement in English, "The spirit is willing but the flesh is weak." The second computer translated it into French, "The wine is ready but the meat is spoiled." Something was lost in that translation.

Bible translators and copyists were marvelously accurate in transmitting the scriptures. The famous Dead Sea Scrolls, containing some of the earliest portions of the Old Testament yet discovered, revealed that only minute copyists' errors had crept in through the ages. At the same time our English Bibles are only translations of the original Hebrew, Aramaic, and Greek, and sometimes, meanings have gotten lost in translation.

The Bible Is a True Record

When I was much younger I was greatly concerned lest some verbal error might be found in the Bible, thus discounting biblical truth. This would have rocked my faith, for instead of a well-grounded faith in God, I had linked my faith to the Bible's inerrancy. I had fallen victim to the heresy of worshiping the Bible instead of God.

As my faith and trust in God grew, the need for verbal infallibility grew less and less. At the same time, I have become more and more certain that the Bible's message is true! God loves us; Christ died and rose again; we are forgiven; eternal life is a reality. This is the heart of the Bible's message.

It is important to remember that the idea of God developed gradually throughout the Old Testament. One of England's greatest preachers and authors, Dr. Leslie D. Weatherhead, writes:

Taking the Bible as we have it, it begins with a local storm god who lives on the top of Mr. Sinai, and when the Israelites get too far from the mountain he has to be carried with them. The smoke of the burning censer, symbolizing the Divine Presence, is seen in daylight as a pillar of cloud, and at night the smoke is lit up by the burning wood and looks like a pillar of fire. Only so can the people be made to believe that their God has not been left behind like the gods of Egypt!

Even when he gets the Israelites to Canaan, by a method of invasion on the same moral level as the rape of Ethiopia by the Italians, or of Hungary by the Russians (save that the latter, in both cases, did not pretend it was the will of God!), he remains a jealous, vindictive tyrant, punishing the children for their fathers' sins and thinking nothing of turning a terrified woman into a pillar of salt, ordering massacres, having a helpless old man hacked in pieces before him, or visiting his devoted servant Job with disease and pain until he longed for death. (*The Christian Agnostic*, Abingdon Press, 1965)

The Divine Plan

Other theologians take a more conservative view. They find justification, for instance, for the slaughter of the Canaanites. A friend of mine, a very knowledgable Bible student, gives this traditional view:

The basic reason for God's command to exterminate the Canaanites was to keep the Israelites from becoming contaminated by the religion and morals of the inhabitants of Canaan (Exodus 23:23; 34:13; Deuteronomy 7). It should be noted that in actuality the Israelites never did fully carry out the command, and as a result, they were continually drawn away from God and involved in the immoral religious practices of the inhabitants.

The appalling moral degradation of the Canaanites is undeniable. Their religion involved the sacrifices of their first-born infants to the god Moloch, temple prostitution, and numerous other abominations.

However, a great many theologians lean somewhat more to Weatherhead's view.

The Israelites were selected by God for earth's most important mission—to transmit to the rest of the world the concept of monotheism and an enlightened ethical and moral code. They were to be a light to the

Gentiles, and the climax of their mission was to bring forth and accept the Messiah.

As it turned out, they were little better than their neighbors. But a tiny minority *worried* about it, the prophets, who kept calling Israel back to the one true God.

The God portrayed at the beginning of the Old Testament is not the God of the New Testament as I understand him. There has been a progressive revelation of God culminating in a loving heavenly Father, revealed in Jesus. God is always the same but humans can only see a minuscule part of him. The primitive Israelites saw an angry, punitive deity. They had no basis for conceiving the loving God of the New Testament. As revelation progressed the later prophets began to proclaim the love of God and his concern for the whole world.

John Wesley insisted on an expurgated edition of the Psalms, writing in the preface: "Many Psalms are left out and many parts of others are highly improper for the mouths of a Christian congregation." He omitted the murderous Psalm 137 and Psalm 139:19-22 among others.

The church excluded from public worship the reading of the Old Testament in the fifth century, in view of the fact that it justifies the stoning of blasphemers and adulteresses (but not adulterers) and contained so much slaughter presumably ordered by God.

Many ministers and Christian educators take strong exception to using many parts of the Old Testament as material suitable for teaching children, particularly the bloodier portions, and the incidents that seem to place

God's stamp of approval on less than Christian attitudes.

Was it God's command that Joshua kill twelve thousand men, women, and children in Ai, saving only the cattle from destruction? Was it God's intent that the Israelites destroy every living soul—men, women, and children—in Lachish, Libnah, Jericho, and Gezer?

Many Christians find it difficult to believe that God commanded Samuel to continue the slaughter begun by Moses and Joshua. He destroyed the Amalekites, whose king was Agag: "And Samuel hewed Agag in pieces before the Lord in Gilgal" (I Sam. 15:33*b*). Must we believe that this bloody massacre was the will of God? Were the Israelites mistaken about God's commands?

In all of their battles the Hebrews carried the Ark of the Covenant with them in which was presumably the essence of God. This God whom they carried with them was so terrible that when some curious people peeked in he "killed seventy of the men" (I Sam. 6:19 TLB).

For instance, in the second chapter of II Kings, it is recorded that Elisha was headed toward Bethel, when he encountered a large group of children, who began to mock him. "Go up, thou bald head, go up, thou bald head." Elisha, stung by their ridicule, "cursed them in the name of the Lord," whereupon two female bears came out of the adjacent woods and killed and ate forty-two of them (II Kings 2:23-24 KJV).

A careful Bible student has pointed out that "the event took place at Bethel, the seat of calf worship; that the phrase translated 'little children' in the KJV would better be translated 'young men.' The same term is used of Solomon as a young man in I Kings 3:7. The import of their statement is 'go away that we be unreproved in our evil ways.' It would seem from the large number injured that the group was more like a hostile, surly mob. The severity of the judgment is accounted for by the fact that in being derisive to and rejecting God's appointed spokesman they were in effect rejecting him." All other considerations aside, it does seem that forty-two children—or young men—are quite a lot for two bears to consume.

Those were primitive days. Christian love and compassion were not to be preached for many centuries. God had to work with what he had. But a casual reading of this account would seem to imply that Elisha was justified in cursing the children for their impudence, and that God sent the bears to kill the children in response to Elisha's having pronounced a curse on them.

A little girl, reading some Old Testament events that struck her as particularly brutal, said in explanation, "That must have been before God became a Christian." Some Old Testament accounts, if taken literally, would seem to validate that idea.

Some Moral Problems

We read in I Chronicles that David decided to take a census. It is stated that the idea was Satanic in origin, and for some reason contrary to the will of God. After the census was taken, "The Lord sent a plague upon Israel and 70,000 men died as a result. During the plague God sent an angel to destroy Jerusalem; but then he felt such compassion that he changed his mind and commanded the destroying angel, 'Stop! It is enough!' " (I Chron. 21:14-15 TLB).

On the basis of the facts as stated, it would seem strange that the taking of a census could so provoke God that he would exact vengeance and kill 70,000 men; that he would decide to destroy Jerusalem, and then, as though repenting of his impetuosity, order the angel of death to desist. This poses some problems.

First, it was David who reportedly sinned in taking the census, but he was not punished. Second, 70,000 presumably innocent men died in the plague supposedly sent by God. God does not send plagues, but in those ancient days all disasters were believed to be God's punishment.

Then, there are the moral problems involved in some of the Psalms. David's prayers asking God to slay his enemies and to bless those who would smash Babylonian babies against the rocks (Psalm 137) leave us wondering. One possible answer, of course, is that the psalmist, in complete honesty with his emotions, "lets it all hang out," expresses what he is feeling at the moment—which is good therapy—and later comes up with a more charitable reaction. In some of his more vehement psalms the author excoriates his enemies with intense hatred, then at the end, his violence spent, he praises God. But to a casual reader, the imprecatory psalms seem bloodthirsty.

Psalm 91 says: "A thousand shall fall at thy side, and ten thousand at thy right hand; but it shall not come nigh thee" (v. 7 KJV). The Christians martyred during the Roman persecution, and the uncounted millions of faithful believers since then who have suffered disease, death, and disasters make us realize that the psalmist who wrote that exultant statement could not have been speaking for the God they loved and believed in.

I have asked scores of ministers, and many ardent Bible students, if they remember the climax of the Book of Esther. I have found no one who can recall its strange and terrible ending.

King Ahasuerus (another name of Xerxes) of Persia, was the most powerful monarch of the ancient world. He ruled Persia from 485-465 B.C.

At a great banquet given for his nobles held in preparation for his forthcoming expedition against Greece, in which he fought the battle of Thermopylae, he ordered Queen Vashti to appear before his guests to display her beauty. She refused. On the advice of the king's counselors, she was deposed, lest feminism sweep the land.

A vast number of beautiful maidens were rounded up from far and near, from among whom the king would choose a successor to Vashti. Among the candidates was Esther, a Jewish orphan, who had been reared by Mordecai, a relative. Esther was chosen to be the new queen.

Mordecai proudly refused to bow to Haman, the king's prime minister, who then plotted to have all the Jews of the kingdom destroyed. At Haman's insistence, the king ordered that the Jews be exterminated.

Learning of the plot, Queen Esther pleaded with the king, who gave an order saving the Jews and authorizing them to retaliate against their enemies.

The Sunday school moral, quite appropriately, is that brave Queen Esther saved her people. What is interesting is that virtually everyone, by some peculiar selective memory, fails to recall that the next day the

Jews went out and *joyfully slaughtered seventy-five thousand of their Gentile enemies* (Esther 9:16). Also forgotten is the fact that Esther saw to it that not only was Haman hanged, but that *all ten of his sons*— presumably innocent—were also hanged (Esther 9:12). Attention is called to this, not to discredit Esther's splendid role in saving her people, but in the interest of historical accuracy.

What About Inconsistencies?

A few inconsistencies appear to be in some of the biblical writings which we may as well face. Some of them are due to faulty translations, the errors of copyists, or conceivably different authors seeing the same event from a different angle. The basic truth remains—*do not doubt that!*—but honesty compels us to face the reality that there are apparent minor discrepancies.

Second Samuel 10:18 records that David slew the men of seven *hundred* Syrian chariots. First Chronicles 19:18 tells us that David slew the men of seven *thousand* Syrian chariots. This is undoubtedly a copyist's error.

In II Samuel 24:1 we read that it was the *Lord* who commanded David to take a census of Israel. First Chronicles 21 tells us that it was *Satan*. Perhaps there is some way to resolve this apparent contradiction, but it poses a problem to the reader.

In calling attention to those apparent instances I do not discredit biblical truth. A dozen people or a hundred for that matter describing the same event will mention different aspects of the happening. Someone reading the varying accounts might surmise that they are describing entirely different events; but *there would be truth in each account,* as perceived by the observer. But we do not do ourselves a favor if we ignore such inconsistencies or pretend they do not exist.

There are other instances: Jehu exterminated the house of Ahab, in the territory of Jezreel, and in II Kings 10:30, the Lord *congratulates* Jehu on having done so. In Hosea 1:4 the Lord *condemns* the house of Jehu for shedding the blood of Jezreel. It is seemingly impossible to reconcile these two concepts.

There are numerous other conflicts which over-zealous defenders of the Bible's inerrancy have sought to reconcile. Instead of laboring so painfully toward a reconciliation of all the apparent inconsistencies, I much prefer the attitude of C. S. Lewis, who believed that "the kind of truth we demand of Scriptures was, in my opinion, never ever envisaged by the ancients" (Michael J. Christenson, *C. S. Lewis on Scripture,* Word, 1979).

Dr. Harry Ironside, who was pastor some years ago of the very conservative Moody Church in Chicago, was quoted in a publication of *Evangelicals Concerned* as saying, "God, who is love, is more concerned that his people walk in love toward another, than that they contend valiantly for set forms of truth, however scriptural."

Jesus Christ Is the Touchstone

I have spent time on these problem areas of the Bible, for two reasons. First, we need to recognize that just because something is in the Bible doesn't mean we should emulate it or that it is applicable to us today. *Jesus Christ is the touchstone by which we test all that claims to be truth.* The Bible records truly what happened—so that we see the Israelites as pre-Christian. But because we know Jesus Christ, we do not stone sinners, and we are not commanded to wipe out enemies. Second, as I have already said, if we do not honestly deal with the problem areas in the Bible, we are not being true followers of Jesus who said, "I am . . . the truth."

The central theme of the Bible is the promise of the Messiah: the expectation of his coming, his birth, life and atoning death, and final triumphant reign.

Something about him transcends denominational differences, culture, race, and a thousand petty distinctions. He demonstrates unconditional, redemptive love, and tells us that God is like that. His revelation transforms the Old Testament, shedding a brilliant light on the hints of God's love hidden there.

We could wish that we knew what he looked like, more of what he taught, for the record is really quite sketchy. And yet, those glimpses we have of him are magnificent, glorious. They challenge and confront us, while his love forgives and comforts us. He ignores nationality and religious distinctions. He converses at a well with a woman of shabby morals and reveals for the first time that he is the Messiah—yes, to this five-times-married woman living with a sixth man to whom she is not married.

He knelt and looked into the face of a terrified woman and did not bother to tell her that she was forgiven; she could see that in his eyes. He invited himself to dinner in the homes of despised tax collectors; he dealt ever so gently with a prostitute who rained tears on his feet. This is God incarnate.

[163]

Long centuries ago, Bernard of Clairvaux (it is thought) wrote the simple but lovely words of a hymn which we still sing:

> Jesus, the very thought of thee
> With sweetness fills my breast;
> But sweeter far thy face to see,
> And in thy presence rest.

It is he, Son of man, Son of God, the Living Christ, whom we love and serve.

12

The Church

If we traverse the world, it is possible to find cities without walls, without letters, without kings, without wealth, without coin, without schools and theatres, but a city without a temple or that practiceth not worship and prayers, no one ever saw.

—*Plutarch*

Plutarch's comment quoted at the head of this chapter was made nineteen centuries ago, but it is still largely true.

I have visited the pyramids of Egypt, Chitzen Itza, Teotihuacan, Puebla and Tikal, in Guatemala. I have crawled over the ruins of Machu Picchu, Knossos, Luxor, Baalbek, and Corinth. I have seen the ruined temples of ancient Greece, Jerash, Babylon, the Acropolis, Petra, and Ephesus.

All of them except Machu Picchu and Knossos have archaeological ruins of temples or religious centers, and it is quite possible that in those two cities were temples that may have long since vanished.

Man is incurably religious. The pagan temples of Katmandu and Bangkok, with their sculpted scowling mythological beasts guarding the entrance, tell us that, however faulty their concept of God, people will always worship.

Sigmund Freud assured us that "religion is the universal neurosis of humanity; like the obsessional neurosis of children, it arose out of the Oedipus complex, out of the relation to the father" (*The Future of an Illusion*, edited by James Strachey, W. W. Norton & Co., 1975).

He argues that in time humankind will surmount this neurotic phase, just as many children outgrow their similar neurosis. Children, feeling weak and vulnerable, turn their parents into gods. Man makes a god in the image of his parents, particularly father, and then makes promises to the god, in an effort to win special favors or protection, according to Freud. Religion, he insists, was born because people needed to make their helplessness tolerable. They build up from the memories of their childhood helplessness, the need for a superparent, a god. Both the Jew Karl Marx and the Jew Sigmund Freud attempted to destroy belief in the Jew Jesus.

Against the teaching of Freud there is Jesus' teaching.

For more than half a century, I have been a Christian minister. Contrary to Freud, I believe implicitly the statement of Jesus concerning his church, "Not even death will ever be able to overcome it" (Matt. 16:18*b* TEV). I love the church and feel very defensive when it is criticized by an outsider, feeling perhaps illogically that only we who love it have a right to discuss its faults. Certainly we are the only ones who can balance the church's virtues and strengths against its failures. If I point out some of the church's weaknesses in this chapter, it is out of loving concern for the future welfare of earth's only deathless institution.

When You Lose Power, Organize?

There is an ancient legend to the effect that the Devil and a friend were walking down the street one day when, some distance away, they saw a man stoop down, pick up something, and put it in his pocket. The friend asked, "What was that he picked up?"

"He picked up a piece of truth."

"That's a bad business for you, then."

"Not at all," responded the Devil casually. "I'll encourage him to organize it, and that will be the end of its power."

There is a disturbing germ of truth in that story. The early church had tremendous power, and very little organization. During the first three hundred years, the church grew faster than at any time since. But when Constantine legalized the church in A.D. 325, the dynamic little groups of worshipers disbanded their small home churches and organized into large congregations. From then on their growth was much slower. From multitudes of small loving groups of people worshiping and serving, the church became a great organized hierarchy.

Two Christians in one day told me with some bitterness of their disillusionment. One said, "I'm fed up. I went to my church this morning and the minister talked for thirty-five minutes about the importance of attending church. Good grief! *We* were there! He was talking to the wrong people." Another said, "I haven't been attending church lately, but suddenly I found myself wanting to establish a deeper relationship with

God. I went to church, longing for a renewal of my faith, some kind of inspiration; but what a letdown! The service was dull, the hymns dragged, the sermon was in no way related to life. I went out feeling terribly disappointed. I don't know where to turn."

The church seems at times to be a nagging wife instead of the loving bride of Christ, a tradition-encrusted hierarchy whose energies are devoted more to survival than revival or renewal. The liberal, social action-oriented church too often has little to offer its constituents except a new program for improved race relations, peace drives, and ecological crusades. Good as this is—and it is good—it does nothing for the lonely, the bereaved, the warring family, or the individual alienated from himself, from God, and from his neighbor.

At the other end of the theological spectrum are the extremely conservative churches, with their deadly legalism and moralistic approach to life. They provide the terribly insecure individual with the security of a dogmatic set of beliefs and religious clichés.

In the middle, reaching out feebly in either direction are the puzzled mainline churches, not certain just where to place the emphasis. Their dilemma is in not knowing how much of their energies to expend excoriating evildoers, promoting good works in the community, visiting the sick and lonely, engaging in evangelism, or supporting the drug abuse crusade. Some are establishing marriage renewal retreats and trying new approaches to Bible study. Others stress youth activities and choirs for all ages, social activities for single adults, and study groups for those interested in social action.

The Minister's Dilemma

The worshiper who may have just complaints about the relevance of his or her church to modern society, and who would like some change, is usually unaware of the dilemma confronting the minister. The minister must be a preacher, teacher, businessman, fund raiser, entertainer, prophet, priest, friend of children, counselor, supporter of the women's society, evangelist and public relations expert. He or she needs a sense of humor, but should be dignified and poised. The minister's children should set an example for all the children of the congregation, and his or her marriage is presumed to be idyllic, despite the fact that he or she may spend from five to seven nights a week away from home.

As a minister, I have been phoned innumerable times—often by members of other churches—to help them find a baby-sitter, or a companion for some elderly relative (a nice room and meals with no salary in exchange for full-time nursing and housekeeping). Many ministers are deluged with requests to find jobs, often for unemployables. And then there are the pitiful letters from mothers in distant cities: "Please visit my son living near you. He left the church many years ago, and is drinking to excess. He and his wife are divorcing. Try to get him to attend church, but don't let him know I wrote you. He lives only about fifty miles from you."

The minister is often caught between the "in thing" being promoted this season by the denomination, the needs of individuals in the congregation, and the demands placed on him or her by the community. With their sixty-hour week, ministers belong to one of the poorest paid of all professions. They could spend all of their time in visitation and counseling, leaving ten other areas untended; or they could devote half of their time to administration and half to social action causes, still feeling frustrated over neglecting youth, the shut-ins, counseling, and study. Funerals and weddings need to be fitted in some place. Many clergy are harrassed victims, puzzled prophets, and frustrated preachers.

The apostle Paul would never have made it in a modern church. The Reverend Norman R. De Puy writes:

For one thing he suffered from some obnoxious disease and had bad eyes. Strike one. Every pulpit committee wants to know about a prospective pastor's health. . . . Paul would never qualify.

For another thing he was not attractive physically. No wavy hair or beautiful smile . . . He had a poor work record. He didn't stay very long, and with most of the churches he had a running battle . . . while there.

He [seems] incredibly vain by any popular standard. He talks of "my gospel," and tells people if they want to know what a Christian is all they have to do is look at him. . . .

The apostle told the people of Galatia if they were so all-fired interested in circumcision, they ought to cut the whole business off. That's crude and intemperate. That's like saying to Baptists, if you like baptism so much, go drown yourselves. He also told the troublemakers in Galatia to go to hell—twice, in two consecutive verses, in case they didn't get it the first time. He was not cussing; he meant hell—theological, biblical hell. They should definitely go there, he said, if they were going to preach differently from him. Very coarse.

[It will be argued that] he made up for all of his shortcomings with a brilliant mind, and passionate soul, and therefore justly deserves his status as the church's number one theologian and evangelist.

But I stick to my original statement: I don't think he could get work in our present day churches. His theology was radical, revolutionary . . . and extremely demanding. . . .

He would brook no compromise: a little sentiment, a little cultural religion, something nice for the old folks or the young folks? No! Either Christ or nothing. (*The American Baptist*, July-August, 1976)

The Church and Money

As an insider viewing the beloved church and its faults, I need to mention church financing. Years ago when I assumed the pastorate of a church suffering from some financial problems, I found that the women of the church had been raising money with cake sales, rummage sales, and the like. When I instituted the writing of a new church constitution which stated that there would be no such fund raising, a dear woman much devoted to such affairs, tackled me on the matter. "We just give and give until we can't give any more," she said. "We must use these methods to support the church." Admitting that church bazaars can be fun (playing store) and avoids having to raise one's pledge to the church, I said, "If by this time next year our budget has not doubled, I will aid you in holding the greatest church bazaar this community has ever had." She settled for that.

Later I looked up the record of her giving. She and her husband, a moderately prosperous man, pledged a dollar a week. With a modern financial program instituted, our budget more than doubled within the year, and we had no need of catch-penny methods of church financing.

Not too long ago I was in the hospital recovering from major surgery. A nurse asked me what my vocation was. I told her that I was a retired minister, that I had been directing a counseling center for some ten years, and that I also wrote books about religion and psychology.

She said, "Oh, religion! I have no use for the churches. All they ever talk about is money. I think the churches are just leeches . . ." She continued for some time with her angry tirade.

I had neither the energy nor the inclination to argue with her. No one has ever talked a person out of such convictions, because they are rooted in neurosis, and one does not talk a person out of a neurosis.

Some of the Church's Shortcomings

Surveys show that in a typical church: 10 percent of the membership do 90 percent of the work, 40 percent attend every Sunday, and 30 percent give 90 percent of the budget. That is about the same proportion of serving and giving to be found in any other organization.

A musicologist could probably explain why so many hymns are unsingable by most of the males in the congregation. A good 90 percent of males have either a baritone or bass voice, and most of them cannot read music. Hence, they are forced to sing an octave lower on most hymns, rumbling along self-consciously while the sopranos and tenors are singing their hearts out. This is not conducive to a good worship experience for a majority of the men in a typical congregation.

[172]

Andrew Greeley, a Roman Catholic priest, columnist and author, writes:

Why is it that organized religion always has to be so creepy?

St. Teresa once prayed: "From silly devotions and sour-faced saints, liber nos Domine (Deliver us, O Lord)."

The Boss, for reasons of his own, doesn't seem to have heard her prayer. It's a real mystery—religious founders and reformers are exciting, enthusiastic men and women. Religion always starts as "good news." It appeals in its early years to the most exciting and adventurous men and women of their generation. But in short order it turns dull, somber and turgid. Try attending a convention of clergy, or picking up the latest issue of a magazine devoted to religion . . . .

Many of the psalms are filled with admonitions to praise God with harp and timbrel, to serve him with joy and gladness, to "Clap your hands all ye people, shout unto God with the voice of triumph. Sing praises to God, sing praises unto our King." (*San Francisco Chronicle*)

But traditional churches take a very dim view of such enthusiastic ways of praising God.

When Christianity is allowed to degenerate into a legalistic system dealing in minutiae of conduct and a long list of prohibitions, it has gone far afield from the major emphasis of Jesus. He spoke of love, joy, peace, happiness, life abundant, and life eternal. This was the good news! A number of churches are majoring on minors, casting a pall of gloom over the landscape, rather than infecting society with the glorious good news of the gospel, which is that God loves us, forgives us, welcomes us, and wants us to rejoice.

I once attended a convention of Christians, most of whom belonged to a rather legalistic denomination. The women wore no makeup whatever, and their hair was in most instances tied back into a severe bun. Most of the men wore fixed plastic smiles and rather ill-fitting clothes. A friend of mine, viewing the scene, said, "I believe there is a market here for what could be called a 'Bible Believer's Home Beauty Kit, with Vitamin E.' "

Clothes and makeup are relatively unimportant parts of life, but when Christians go to great effort to look only their most solemn and shabby, they are poor witnesses to the joyous Christ who held out his arms in invitation to the tired and lonely, the sick, the lame, and the discouraged, inviting them into the kingdom of love, joy, and peace.

The Church Is Christ's Body

The church, with all of its human weaknesses, is divine. I love it. It has a glorious future. It will never die. We have that on the promise of Jesus. And I know many churches where the services are joyous affairs, with people welcoming and loving one another, generating a spirit of Christian fellowship that must be akin to that of the early church.

When Jesus walked the earth in the flesh, he could hold out his arms in a loving welcome and invite the sick and troubled to come to him. When he left the earth, he assigned this task to us. Christ now has no arms but ours, no voice but our voices, no physical expression of love or compassion except that which we manifest. It is sobering and challenging to realize that, faulty as we are, we are Christ's authorized representatives on earth.

If you have not found a local church that fits your needs, don't become discouraged or disillusioned. Shop around until you find one that suits your temperament and spiritual requirements. Join it! Serve through it! Become an active part of the living Body of Christ which is deathless.

13

Love, Divine and Human

Some day, after we have mastered the winds, the waves, the tides and gravity we will harness for God the energies of love, and then for the second time in history of the world man will have discovered fire.
—*Pierre Teilhard De Chardin, S.J.*

Dr. Paul Warner writes:

A friend of mine was staying overnight in the home of a Yugoslav pastor, his wife and three boys. . . . Two of the boys were handsome, strong young men. They were going to the university and showing high promise. The third boy, twenty years old, was over in the corner of the room playing with his toys. My friend asked if he might take a picture of the family, thinking of the parents and the two normal boys. But the father said to him, "Wait a moment until I get him ready."

Then the picture was taken with the retarded boy in the center. My friend said to me, "Never show that picture to anyone. We can't exploit human tragedy." But I learned something from that father about what it meant to belong to the family. No child was missing from that picture, not one.

You and I belong to the Father's family. And not one of us is missing from that picture, not one. Each of us feels at times the idiot in himself, feels himself to be ugly, unacceptable, loathsome, outcast. But you and I are in the center of that picture, just as we are, beloved by the Father. Let us feel now that inner power moving in us, like an inner tidal wave singing affirmation, "Yes, I'm with you and for you. I love you, you beautiful idiot, you." (*Feeling Good About Feeling Bad*, Word, 1979)

Who among us has not felt the idiot, the unlovable bungler?

If we do not love ourselves properly, we cannot readily accept God's love. No matter how many sermons we hear about the matchless love of God, if we do not accept and love ourselves properly, we have difficulty in feeling worthy of divine love.

When No One Listens

Randy, a young man of thirty-two, had come to our counseling center for intensive therapy, in an effort to resolve his lifelong depression. In one Primal Integration session he relived a typical family scene as a small boy. There was incessant screaming and fighting, not only between the children, but between the parents as well.

But Randy's chief complaint was that no one ever listened to him, or expressed any interest in what he had to say. "I didn't count, and I still don't," he said. "People just don't care enough to listen."

In an effort to help him accept the fact that many people are not good listeners, I pointed out that most humans are self-centered. "They are more concerned about themselves, their ideas, and their feelings, than the problems of anyone else," I said. "We are all egocentric. Your toothache is of more concern to you, for instance, than the fact that two billion people will go to bed hungry tonight."

Randy suddenly became very hostile. "Don't say that! I don't want to hear it!" I was glad of the intensity of his response, for it is impossible to be both angry and depressed at the same time. "I don't want it that way," he said. "It's not right; it's all wrong. People should listen!"

"Right," I said, "but they don't. They want to talk. They want *you* to listen. That's the way the world operates. It's rotten, but it's reality."

Randy then went into a rage. It was the emotional response we had been searching for, anger at his parents for never listening, for being so obsessed with their own problems that they had no time to be concerned with his feelings. The releasing of his anger was the beginning of his cure.

The child who is never listened to, nor affirmed, derives a feeling that "I'm worthless; no one pays any attention to me, I'm no good." Thus the basis for self-hate is formed. And if persons cannot accept and love themselves properly, they neither love others, nor can they accept love. They do not feel worthy. Anger over this, deeply repressed, usually results in some form of depression.

How Do We Love Ourselves?

Sören Kierkegaard wrote:

When the commandment "to love one's neighbor" is rightly understood, it also says the converse, "Thou shalt love thyself in the right way." If anyone, therefore, will not learn from Christianity to love himself in the right way, then neither can he love his neighbor. He may perhaps . . . cling to one of several other human beings, but this is by no means loving one's neighbor. To love oneself in the right way, and to love one's neighbor, are absolutely analogous concepts, and are at bottom the one and the same. (*Works of Love*, trans. David Swenson, Harper & Row, 1962)

The tragedy, of course, is that when persons understand intellectually that they should love themselves properly, this does not automatically enable them to do so. They do not know how. They simply feel unlovable. If they were not loved as children, in a manner they could accept, then during those formative years they began to reject themselves, to despise their very being. How, then, do people learn to love themselves?

If one were loved and affirmed as a child, it is much easier for such a person to reach the goal of loving God, himself or herself and others. But if there was a severe deprivation of love, in the form of holding, cuddling, and affirmation, then no amount of reading or listening to sermons will provide a solution.

No amount of verbal assurance, "See how much we love you," outweighs the day-by-day verbal assaults: "Look at your clothes! Clean yourself up, this instant." "Stop that, do you hear me? I won't put up with it another minute!" "You'll be the death of me yet," "God doesn't love you when you're bad," or any of a thousand variations on the theme. The message the child receives is "You despise me; I'm worthless. No one can ever love me."

Unconditional Love

There is another complex aspect to this. Sometimes loving parents, longing for a child's best, can unwittingly set the stage for self-rejection. The story of Katie, told by her mother, Margaret Stern Mattisson, in *Reader's Digest* some time ago, illustrates this:

Katie was "bright, loving, popular, successful—'perfect,' we felt, in every way. And then one awful night, she tried to end her life."

One evening when the mother was at the church practicing for the production of a musical in which she had a part, Katie phoned her: "Mother, come home . . . I've taken sleeping . . . sleeping . . . sleep . . ." There was a crash as Katie dropped the phone. The mother rushed home, and Katie was taken to the hospital. The father and mother sat beside her as Katie slowly regained consciousness. They asked themselves the agonizing questions, Why? What went wrong?

When Katie began to revive, she exhibited venemous anger, using violent epithets and vulgar expressions that shocked her parents. Katie had never sworn before, or used such gutter language. She lashed out at the nurse, snapping like an animal, and bloodied the nose of an intern. There were kicks and angry screams.

Much later, when Katie awoke from her sedated sleep she whispered, "I sort of remember. . . . I hated everything, everything."

"Us, Katie, mostly us?" Katie's father asked.

"No, mostly me," she said, closing her eyes.

The staff psychiatrist later reported to the parents that Katie was a very confused and bewildered young woman, who really hated herself.

The mother insisted, "But she's wonderful—always has been. She must know it!"

The doctor replied, "She knew you thought so, and she tried to be, felt she *had* to be what you thought she was. That's what she was telling us last night. . . . She didn't want to disappoint you—didn't want anyone to think she wasn't as nice as they all thought she was. We all want to be loved, you know. She thought acting nice was what made people love her—even her parents. She doesn't think she is a person, so dying doesn't matter."

The parents insisted that they had aways loved Katie. How was it possible that she could hate herself. The psychiatrist replied, "Love is not enough. You can't exist as the reflection of someone's love. You have to be your own person."

While Katie was dutifully presenting herself to the world, and chiefly to her parents, as the ideal daughter, she harbored a secret, seething self-contempt. She didn't feel she measured up. She had climbed up onto the pedestal her loving parents had built for her, but she couldn't sustain the false image. She kept on playing the role of a loving, dutiful, sweet, successful daughter until the burden became too great. The price of being loved was to play the role.

This story, told by the mother, is a powerful reminder that love must be unconditional. It must not be, "We love you when you are good, or succeed, or get good grades, or have a clean room, or look nice, or reach the goals we set for you." The child must be loved when acting contrary to all the rules, when insolent, or rebellious. The difficulty, of course, is that the child needs love the most when being the least lovable. And when a parent is feeling frustrated and angry, and a miserable failure, hostility toward the child is likely to erupt. Such anger is usually based on not knowing how to get the desired results and a sense of parental failure.

Love Is More Than a Feeling

We are prone to think of love as an emotion. When Jesus commands us to love our enemies, we tend to ignore this seemingly impossible admonition because we simply don't feel loving toward the despicable people who have injured us. But Jesus is not asking us to feel affection, or liking, for such people. We are called on to express good will. Anyone can love charming, pleasant, gracious, well-integrated people. That is no problem. Jesus asks the seeming impossible—that we express unconditional good will—*agapē*-love*—for the unpleasant people whom we instinctively dislike, since they are so disagreeable. He gave us an example when he uttered those memorable words from the cross, "Father, forgive them; for they know not what they do" (Luke 23:34). Here is the example, to match the command.

Linked with this is the command to "pray for those who persecute you" (Matt. 5:44). This, we concede, is not easy. In fact, it is one of the most difficult things Jesus ever asked us to do—to love our enemies *and* pray for them. It is far easier to join a protest march, or castigate evildoers, or contend passionately for the verbal inspiration of the Bible, or some other cherished religious doctrine, than it is to pray for one's enemies. But until we have made a heroic effort to comply with this fundamental command of Jesus, we have little reason to call ourselves his followers.

Jesus firmly linked our being forgiven with our willingness to forgive others. It is not that God withholds his forgiveness until we meet his conditions. He is, by his very nature, unable to give to us

---

*Agapē is the Greek word the New Testament writers used for God's love demonstrated in Jesus Christ. It is a love not based on the beauty or worthiness of the object of love, but solely on the decision of the lover. Carl Rogers, psychologist, defines it as "unconditional positive concern."

what we will not share with others. So, if you want to be forgiven, then you must learn to forgive, and—as Jesus stipulated—it must not be just a verbal forgiveness; it must be "from the heart." This implies a total, wholehearted erasure of bitterness and resentment.

How can one express this *agapē*-love Jesus keeps insisting upon?

Dr. Paul Tournier expresses it quite succinctly:

Love is not just some great abstract idea or feeling. There are some people with such a lofty conception of love that they never succeed in expressing it in the simple kindness of ordinary life. They dream of heroic devotion and self-sacrificing service. But waiting for the opportunity which never comes, they make themselves very unlikable to those near them, and never sense their neighbor's need.

To love is to will good for another. Love may mean writing with enough care so that our correspondent can read without spending time deciphering: that is, it may mean taking the time to save his time. To love is to pay one's bills; it is to keep things in order so a wife's work will be made easier. It means arriving somewhere on time; it means giving your full attention to the one who is talking to you. (*Guilt and Grace,* Harper & Row, 1962)

How often have you begun to share something important with a friend or acquaintance, and have had the conversation snatched from you with something like, "Yes, now take me for instance. Last week . . ." We are quite rightly irritated, or at least disappointed, at not being listened to. We feel that if our friends really cared they would listen.

Love implies being willing to listen to another with attention and interest. And if you aren't particularly interested and feel phony when you fake it, remember that it is not hypocritical to act appropriately. We are especially loving when we do a kindness for another when we don't particularly feel like it; for love is not just a feeling, it is an action.

Compulsive talkers are usually people who were not listened to as children. They are making up for lost time. The child who feels unloved because no one pays any attention to him or her may go in either of two directions. The more passive individual retreats into silence; the aggressive one becomes overtalkative. Both are asking for love.

If you want to express love, listen! Restrain the impulse to interject your opinions, or some gem of wisdom. Just manifest interest. If you are not particularly concerned with what is being said, you can be interested in the person's need to be heard. To listen in this manner is to express love.

There is a deep-seated need in all humans for unconditional love, but since it is impossible for anyone to give us this kind of love all the time, most of us end up either disappointed, frustrated, or angry.

Someone tells of a wealthy husband, considerably older than his wife, who asked her if she would still love him if he lost all of his money. She assured him that she would.

"Would you love me if I became an invalid?" he asked.

"Yes, of course."

"But would you still love me if I became blind and deaf?"

"Yes," she said, "I'd still love you."

"But what if I lost all my money, was a blind and deaf invalid, and lost my mind?"

"Don't be ridiculous!" she said. "Who could love an old penniless, blind and deaf imbecile! But I'd take care of you."

The story points up the difficulty of giving unconditional love under impossible conditions, and the human need for it. But the wife's response, "I'd take care of you," indicated her willingness to express *agapē*-love.

Bernice, a dynamic woman of sixty-two, shared with me her discovery that love cannot be forced. She said:

When I was two years old my father abandoned the family. Mother, with a whole batch of kids, had to go to work in a box factory to feed and clothe us. Our father never contributed a dime to our support. I grew to hate him.

Years later I happened to meet him and we established a fairly good relationship, though I had difficulty understanding or forgiving his failure to care for us. He has always been a boozer, drinking steadily throughout the day though never drunk. He was ninety when it appeared that I would be the one to take care of him. I decided two years ago to write and invite him to come and live with me. But I was having mixed feelings. His steady drinking, his foul-smelling cigars, and the fact of my resentment toward him stopped me cold. I felt I was supposed to love him, and felt guilty because I couldn't.

You may recall that I shared this with you two or three years ago, and you said that I was under no obligation to feel affection for him, only *agapē*-love, a kind of unconditional positive regard for him as a human being. That relieved my guilt over not "honoring" my father, which I took for some reason to mean that I had to feel affection for him. As soon as I learned that I didn't have to feel any particular filial affection for him, I felt released. So, soon thereafter, I wrote and invited him to come and live with me. I felt good about it. I knew I could handle it without difficulty. Then he discovered that my brother had a cabin on the coast where he could live, and he decided to go live there. It's wonderful how it's worked out. I got the release from my guilt, and felt okay about having him live with me; then I was relieved to find he wasn't coming after all. He died recently, and for some strange reason I feel a sense of loss. He was a rotten father, but somehow I miss him.

I told her that hers was the kind of love spoken in the thirteenth chapter of First Corinthians, especially the part which reads: "Love keeps no score of wrongs; does not gloat over other men's sins. . . . There is nothing love cannot face; there is no limit to its faith, its hope, and its endurance" (NEB).

Loving Is Good for Us

Jesus did not command love solely because God expects it of us, or because it is good for society, or the other person. Love is good for *us*.

Recent medical discoveries indicate that we are much better off physically and emotionally if we can express love. Dr. Robert B. Greenblatt points this out. His credentials are impressive. He is a member of medical societies in twelve states and nine foreign countries, and has achieved international recognition for his remarkable accomplishments. He has written five hundred and fifty scientific articles and authored ten medical books, among many other accomplishments. In his book, *Search the Scriptures*, he writes: "Kindness, gentleness, tolerance, generosity and charity are ingredients for prevention of, and balm for coronary heart disease."

Being unloving does some drastic things to one's
heart. Dr. Greenblatt refers us to Nabal, an Old
Testament character who was noted for his miserable
disposition and angry outbursts. On one occasion his
lovely wife, Abigail, tried to make amends for him and
thus save his life. When Nabal learned of the threat
against his life, he became enraged and suffered a
heart attack. When he was sober, the account reads,
"His wife told him these things, and his heart died
within him, and he became as a stone" (I Sam. 25:37).
He died ten days later of what Dr. Greenblatt
describes as a coronary attack. "Certain individuals
are more prone to myocardial infarction than others;
those who cannot control emotional responses are
quick to anger, are given to anxiety, fear, avarice,
greed, envy."

When the Bible speaks of a person's heart turning to
stone it is generally assumed that this is hyperbole; but
now a world-famous heart transplant surgeon, Dr.
Denton A. Cooley, of Houston, Texas, has described
"stone heart" as a clinical entity—"a perplexing
phenomenon that occurs during open-heart surgery.
The heart is frozen in a state of contracture—a sort of
rigor mortis of the heart. The Houston team encountered thirteen fatal cases of stone heart in five
thousand open-heart operations."

There are many kinds of love, and this poses a
semantic problem. In our language the word *love* can
refer to a passion for flowers, a liking for chocolate
candy, and sex, romance, parent-child relationships,
and a dozen other emotions.

The Greeks had three frequently used words for
love and half a dozen others to express an affinity, or

attachment, for country, friends, one's fellowman, and relatives.

Our English word *love* is hopelessly inadequate to convey all the semantic connotations that we demand of it. We say: "I just love this dessert." "Do you promise to love, honor, and cherish?" "Come on, prove your love just this once." "I love to travel." "And Jonathan loved David." "So faith, hope, love abide, these three; but the greatest of these is love" (I Cor. 13:13). Then there is "the thundering passion of hormone-drenched adolescents and the quiet affection between grandparents" ("The Science of Love," *Newsweek*, February 25, 1980).

Though varied each of these aspects of love is therapeutic—that is, love of all kinds and description is good for us emotionally and physically. It is both a wonderful preventive and cure, for everything from head colds to cancer, according to recent findings.

Over a period of more than forty years in the ministry, I have performed several thousand marriage ceremonies. Of all the people I married, none ever showed up with a head cold. No bride or groom ever came down with the flu, or any other ailment, for that matter. Love drenches the cells of the body with something marvelously curative.

A Manifestation of God

Every human, both saint and sinner, is an expression of God. No matter how distorted the manifestation may be, that person is a fragment of the divine. The Bible tells us that to fail to love that person is failure to love God.

It is very difficult, at times, to see anything divine in a drunken wretch stumbling along the city streets; or in a child abuser, or a confirmed moral derelict. All we can feel is repugnance. Yet Jesus saw something worthwhile in such outcasts. He fraternized with them and was criticized because he ate in their homes. His gentle acceptance of a prostitute who bathed his feet in her tears, and wiped them with her hair, tells us of his unconditional acceptance of such people. He not only taught *agapē*-love, he demonstrated it.

Many people find it relatively easy to love when there is something in it for them. The case of Mrs. Henrietta Garrett illustrates this. When the eighty-one-year-old childless widow was buried in 1930 in Philadelphia, only about a dozen people were in attendance. Of these only two could be remotely classified as kin. But when it was discovered that she left an estate of some seventeen million dollars, and that no will had been found, Mrs. Garrett became one of the most beloved women in the world. In most of the states of our union, and twenty-nine foreign countries, people began to claim kinship. The estate has now grown to forty million dollars, and more than twenty-six thousand persons have claimed to be heirs. The story of scheming, lying, forgery, perjury, and even violence among the army of missing "heirs" is one of the most interesting in American history.

The heartless greed of the alleged "heirs" is a sorry commentary on human nature, pointing up as it does, the contrast between Mrs. Henrietta Garrett's lonely death and the vicious clamor of twenty-six thousand relatives.

Though not her heirs, we are all related to Mrs.

Garrett, not by blood but because we have a common heavenly Father. We are all related to one another.

In a quite nonrational way, I am saddened by the fact that life is so transitory. I always feel a twinge of disappointment when a beautiful sunset ends, and darkness falls over the once-lovely scene; or when a beautiful child grows into a rather ordinary adult, or when a magnificent symphony plays its last glorious number and the crowd rises to leave. Life's experiences are ephemeral. Spiritual and emotional states are never permanent. But there is one unchanging point. When the last city has crumbled to dust, and all civilization has ended, when "all the works of man shall be destroyed," and the symbols of man's achievements have vanished beneath the final incinerating flash of earth's last hydrogen bomb, there is still a fixed point—the eternal God, who has loved us with an unconditional love.

This is like the "lamp shining in a dark place," as aging Simon Peter put it in a sudden burst of poetic expression, ending, "until the day dawns and the morning star rises in your hearts" (II Pet. 1:19*b*).

Until then, may the God of love and peace grant you the power to love, for love is everything.

Acknowledgments
This page is hereby made a part of the copyright page.

Those noted NIV are from the Holy Bible, New International Version. Copyright © 1978 by New York International Bible Society. Used by permission. Quotations noted TEV (Today's English Version) are from the *Good News Bible*—Old Testament: Copyright © American Bible Society 1976; New Testament: Copyright © American Bible Society 1966, 1971, 1976. The Phillips quotations are from The New Testament in Modern English, copyright © J. B. Phillips 1958, 1960, 1972. Notations indicated KJV are from the King James Version of the Bible.

Quotation on pages 42-43 are copyright 1980 Time Inc. All rights reserved. Reprinted by permission from *Time*.

The quotation on pages 45-46 from *Newsweek* is used by permission of Bill Moyers.

Excerpts on pages 114-16 are taken from *Praising God on the Las Vegas Strip* by Jim Reid. Copyright © 1975 by The Zondervan Corporation. Used by permission.

Excerpts on pages 124-26 are from *Child of Satan, Child of God* by Susan Atkins & Bob Slosser. Copyright © 1976 by Logos Books. Reprinted by permission of Bridge Publishing, Inc., Plainfield, New Jersey 07060.

On pages 131-32 the excerpts from the book *Life After Life* by Raymond A. Moody are used by permission of Mockingbird Books. *Life After Life* has also been published by Bantam Books.

On page 134 the lines from the comic strip Casey are reprinted by permission: Tribune Company Syndicate, Inc.

On pages 170-71 the portions of an article by Dr. Norman R. De Puy which appeared in the July/August 1976 issue of *The American Baptist* are reprinted by permission of *The American Baptist*.

The quoted lines on pages 180-81 are excerpts from "Love Is Not Enough" by Margaret Stern Mattisson, *Reader's Digest*, February 1976. Used by permission.

All names in the personal stories have been changed.